# Contents

# Horchata de Arroz (Rice Drink)

**Prep:** 15 mins **Additional:** 12 hrs **Total:** 12 hrs 15 mins **Servings:** 4 **Yield:** 1 quart

**Ingredients**

- 1 cup uncooked long grain white rice
- 3 ½ cups cold water
- 1 (12 fluid ounce) can evaporated milk
- ½ cup white sugar
- ½ teaspoon ground cinnamon
- 1 teaspoon vanilla extract

**Directions**

**Step 1**

Place the rice in a bowl with enough water to cover it and let it soak overnight.

**Step 2**

Strain the rice and discard the water. Stir the cold water and evaporated milk together. Place the drained rice into a blender along with half of the diluted milk. Blend until the rice is finely ground, about 30 seconds. Add the sugar, cinnamon, and vanilla; blend well. Pour in the remaining diluted milk; blend.

**Step 3**

Line a strainer with two layers of cheesecloth. Place the strainer over another bowl to catch the liquid. Strain the rice milk through the cheesecloth, discard the solids. Repeat the process if necessary. Serve over ice.

**Nutrition Facts**

**Per Serving:**

396 calories; protein 9.7g 20% DV; carbohydrates 71.8g 23% DV; fat 7.5g 12% DV; cholesterol 27.4mg 9% DV; sodium 108.8mg 4% DV.

# Watermelon Delight

Prep: 5 mins Total: 5 mins Servings: 2 Yield: 2 servings

## Ingredients

- 2 cups cubed seeded watermelon
- 5 eaches ice cubes
- 2 tablespoons honey

## Directions

### Step 1

Blend watermelon, ice cubes, and honey in a blender until smooth.

### Nutrition Facts

### Per Serving:

109.4 calories; protein 1g 2% DV; carbohydrates 28.8g 9% DV; fat 0.2g; cholesterolmg; sodium 3.9mg.

# Starbucks Cotton Candy Frappuccino

Prep: 5 mins Total: 5 mins Servings: 1 Yield: 1 beverage

## Ingredients

- 1 ½ cups ice
- ½ cup milk
- ¼ cup vanilla bean powder
- ¾ tablespoon raspberry syrup

## Directions

### Step 1

Blend ice, milk, vanilla powder, and raspberry syrup in a blender until ice is crushed.

### Nutrition Facts

### Per Serving:

325.5 calories; protein 4g 8% DV; carbohydrates 72.2g 23% DV; fat 2.4g 4% DV; cholesterol 9.8mg 3% DV; sodium 61.4mg 3% DV.

# Canary Island Red Mojo Sauce

Prep: 10 mins Total: 10 mins Servings: 20 Yield: 2 1/2 cups

## Ingredients

- 2 large red bell peppers, cut into chunks
- 3 cloves garlic
- 1 tablespoon sweet paprika
- 1 bunch fresh cilantro
- 1 cup olive oil
- 1 chile pepper
- 2 slices bread, crusts removed

## Directions

### Step 1

Blend the bell peppers, garlic, paprika, cilantro, olive oil, chile pepper, and bread in a blender until liquefied.

**Nutrition Facts**

**Per Serving:**

110.4 calories; protein 0.5g 1% DV; carbohydrates 2.9g 1% DV; fat 11g 17% DV; cholesterolmg; sodium 19.5mg 1% DV.

# Easy Blender Salsa

Prep: 15 mins Additional: 30 mins Total: 45 mins Servings: 28 Yield: 28 servings

## Ingredients

- 2 (14.4 ounce) cans diced tomatoes
- 1 jalapeno chile, seeds and ribs removed
- ½ yellow onion, quartered
- ½ bunch cilantro leaves
- 1 tablespoon fresh lemon juice, or to taste
- 1 pinch salt to taste

## Directions

### Step 1

Pour 1 can of tomatoes into a blender, and add the jalapeno pepper, onion, cilantro leaves, lemon juice, and salt. Blend until fairly smooth. Pour in the second can of tomatoes and blend briefly.  seasonings to taste by adding more lemon juice and salt. Let the salsa rest for 1/2 hour before serving to allow the flavors to blend.

**Nutrition Facts**

**Per Serving:**

7.1 calories; protein 0.3g 1% DV; carbohydrates 1.7g 1% DV; fat 0.1g; cholesterolmg; sodium 42.4mg 2% DV.

# Very Berry Blueberry Smoothie

**Prep:** 5 mins **Total:** 5 mins **Servings:** 3 **Yield:** 3 1/2 cups

**Ingredients**

- 1 banana, chopped
- 1 kiwi, sliced
- ¾ cup blueberries
- 1 cup ice cubes
- 1 (8 ounce) container vanilla yogurt

**Directions**

**Step 1**

Combine the banana, kiwi, blueberries, ice cubes, and vanilla yogurt in a blender; blend until smooth.

**Nutrition Facts**

**Per Serving:**

135.4 calories; protein 4.7g 9% DV; carbohydrates 28.4g 9% DV; fat 1.3g 2% DV; cholesterol 3.8mg 1% DV; sodium 53.9mg 2% DV.

# Mango Watermelon Smoothie

**Prep:** 10 mins **Total:** 10 mins **Servings:** 4 **Yield:** 4 servings

**Ingredients**

- 5 cups cubed seeded watermelon
- 1 mango - peeled, seeded, and diced

- ½ cup water
- 1 tablespoon white sugar
- 4 cubes ice cubes

**Directions**

**Step 1**

Blend watermelon, mango, water, and sugar together in a blender until smooth.

**Step 2**

Place ice into glasses and pour smoothie over ice.

**Nutrition Facts**

**Per Serving:**

102.7 calories; protein 1.4g 3% DV; carbohydrates 26.3g 9% DV; fat 0.4g 1% DV; cholesterolmg; sodium 4.5mg.

# Homemade Tomato Juice Cocktail

**Prep:** 10 mins **Additional:** 1 hr **Total:** 1 hr 10 mins **Servings:** 6 **Yield:** 6 servings

**Ingredients**

- 2 cups water
- 1 (6 ounce) can tomato paste
- 2 tablespoons lemon juice
- 2 tablespoons white sugar
- 1 teaspoon salt, or to taste
- 3 cups water, more if needed

**Directions**

**Step 1**

Blend 2 cups water, tomato paste, lemon juice, sugar, and salt together in a blender until smooth; pour into a 1/2 gallon container. Stir 3 cups water into mixture. Refrigerate until thickened, about 1 hour. Add 1 more cup water if juice is too thick.

**Nutrition Facts**

**Per Serving:**

40.6 calories; protein 1.2g 3% DV; carbohydrates 10g 3% DV; fat 0.1g; cholesterolmg; sodium 617.4mg 25% DV.

# Avocado Blueberry Smoothie

**Prep:** 5 mins **Total:** 5 mins **Servings:** 1 **Yield:** 1 smoothie

## Ingredients

- 1 cup frozen blueberries
- 1 (6 ounce) container plain Greek-style yogurt
- ½ cup almond milk
- ½ cup water
- ¼ avocado - peeled, pitted, and diced

## Directions

### Step 1

Blend blueberries, yogurt, almond milk, water, and avocado in a blender until smooth.

**Nutrition Facts**

**Per Serving:**

297.3 calories; protein 11g 22% DV; carbohydrates 39.2g 13% DV; fat 12.3g 19% DV; cholesterol 10.1mg 3% DV; sodium 206.2mg 8% DV.

# Lime-Cilantro Vinaigrette

**Prep:** 10 mins **Total:** 10 mins **Servings:** 12 **Yield:** 1 1/2 cup

## Ingredients

- ¼ cup lime juice
- 2 tablespoons white vinegar
- ½ bunch cilantro, chopped
- 1 tablespoon brown sugar
- 1 clove garlic, minced
- ¼ teaspoon salt
- ¾ teaspoon spicy brown mustard
- ¾ cup light olive oil

## Directions

### Step 1

Blend the lime juice, vinegar, and cilantro together in a blender until smooth. Add the brown sugar, garlic, and salt; blend again until smooth. Spoon the mustard into the mixture. Turn the blender on and slowly pour the olive oil into the dressing mixture in a thin stream; blend until thoroughly combined.

**Nutrition Facts**

**Per Serving:**

126.2 calories; protein 0.1g; carbohydrates 1.7g 1% DV; fat 13.5g 21% DV; cholesterolmg; sodium 54.3mg 2% DV.

# Refreshing Oatmeal Drink (Agua de Avena)

**Prep:** 10 mins **Additional:** 1 hr **Total:** 1 hr 10 mins **Servings:** 8 **Yield:** 8 servings

**Ingredients**

- 8 cups water, divided
- 1 cup quick-cooking oats
- 1 cinnamon stick
- ½ cup white sugar
- 2 teaspoons vanilla extract

**Directions**

**Step 1**

Combine 5 cups water, quick-cooking oats, and cinnamon stick in a blender; blend until combined, about 1 minute.

**Step 2**

Pour the oat mixture through a strainer, collecting the liquids in a pitcher and reserving the solids. Pour remaining water through the strainer containing the solids and into the pitcher. Add sugar and vanilla extract; refrigerate until chilled, about 1 hour.

**Cook's Notes:**

Old fashioned oats can be substituted for quick oats, if desired.

Most of my family enjoys this beverage with a full 1/2 cup of sugar, but it also tastes great with 1/3 cup for those of us who don't like our drinks too sweet.

**Nutrition Facts**

90.9 calories; protein 1.3g 3% DV; carbohydrates 19.8g 6% DV; fat 0.7g 1% DV; cholesterolmg; sodium 7.9mg.

# Wallaby-Darned

**Prep:** 5 mins **Total:** 5 mins **Servings:** 2 **Yield:** 2 cocktails

## Ingredients

- 1 (1.5 fluid ounce) jigger vodka
- 1 (1.5 fluid ounce) jigger peach schnapps
- 1 tablespoon sugar
- ½ cup champagne
- ½ (16 ounce) package frozen sliced peaches
- ½ cup fuzzy navel mix
- 1 cup ice

## Directions

### Step 1

Place the vodka, schnapps, sugar, champagne, peaches, fuzzy navel mix, and ice into a blender. Blend until smooth and serve.

## Nutrition Facts

**Per Serving:**

431 calories; protein 0.8g 2% DV; carbohydrates 78.1g 26% DV; fat 0.2g; cholesterolmg; sodium 14.9mg 1% DV.

# Green Hot Sauce (Salsa Verde)

**Prep:** 15 mins **Cook:** 20 mins **Total:** 35 mins **Servings:** 32 **Yield:** 2 cups

## Ingredients

- 10 medium (blank)s tomatillos, husked and rinsed
- 8 peppers serrano chile peppers, sliced

- 1 onion, sliced
- 1 tablespoon chopped garlic
- 2 tablespoons salt, or to taste

**Directions**

**Step 1**

Place the tomatillos, serrano peppers, onion, and garlic in a saucepan, and add water to just cover. Sprinkle the salt over the top, bring to a boil, reduce the heat to medium-low, and cook until the tomatillos are soft and have turned slightly brownish in color, 20 to 30 minutes. Add more water if needed to keep the mixture from burning as it cooks.

**Step 2**

Pour the cooked vegetables into a blender, and blend until smooth.

**Nutrition Facts**

**Per Serving:**

5.7 calories; protein 0.2g; carbohydrates 1.1g; fat 0.1g; cholesterolmg; sodium 436.5mg 18% DV.

# Strawberry Limeade

**Prep:** 5 mins **Cook:** 5 mins **Total:** 10 mins **Servings:** 6 **Yield:** 6 servings

**Ingredients**

- ½ cup lime juice
- 2 cups cold water
- ¼ cup white sugar
- 1 ½ cups frozen sliced strawberries
- 5 cubes ice

**Directions**

**Step 1**

Place lime juice, cold water, sugar, and strawberries in blender and blend on high until smooth. While blender is running, add ice cubes one at a time.

**Nutrition Facts**

**Per Serving:**

56.7 calories; protein 0.3g 1% DV; carbohydrates 15.1g 5% DV; fat 0.1g; cholesterolmg; sodium 4.4mg.

# Strawberry Shortcake Drink

**Prep:** 5 mins **Total:** 5 mins **Servings:** 1 **Yield:** 1 serving

## Ingredients

- ¼ cup frozen strawberries, thawed
- 1 ¼ fluid ounces amaretto liqueur
- 2 (1/2 cup) scoops vanilla ice cream
- 1 dash vanilla extract
- ½ cup crushed ice
- ¼ fluid ounce vanilla-flavored vodka
- 1 tablespoon whipped cream
- 1 fresh strawberry

## Directions

### Step 1

Place thawed frozen strawberries, amaretto liqueur, vanilla ice cream, vanilla extract, crushed ice, and vanilla vodka into a blender.

### Step 2

Cover and blend until smooth.

### Step 3

Pour into a glass and garnish with whipped cream and a fresh strawberry.

## Nutrition Facts

### Per Serving:

476.3 calories; protein 5.2g 10% DV; carbohydrates 55.4g 18% DV; fat 17.5g 27% DV; cholesterol 68.4mg 23% DV; sodium 112.5mg 5% DV.

# Blended Strawberry Daiquiri

**Prep:** 5 mins **Total:** 5 mins **Servings:** 1 **Yield:** 1 serving

## Ingredients

- 1 cup ice
- 5 eaches strawberries

- 2 fluid ounces white rum
- 1 fluid ounce lime juice
- ½ fluid ounce triple sec
- ½ teaspoon confectioners' sugar

**Directions**

**Step 1**

Blend ice, strawberries, rum, lime juice, triple sec, and confectioners' sugar in a blender at high speed until smooth, about 30 seconds.

**Nutrition Facts**

**Per Serving:**

222.8 calories; protein 0.7g 2% DV; carbohydrates 17.4g 6% DV; fat 0.3g 1% DV; cholesterolmg; sodium 10.5mg.

# Sweet Chipotle Grilling Sauce

**Prep:** 5 mins **Total:** 5 mins **Servings:** 8 **Yield:** 1 cup

**Ingredients**

- 2 peppers chipotle chilies in adobo sauce
- ⅔ cup maple syrup
- 2 cloves garlic, peeled
- 1 tablespoon soy sauce

**Directions**

**Step 1**

Place chilies, maple syrup, garlic, and soy sauce into a blender. Puree until smooth.

**Nutrition Facts**

**Per Serving:**

72.4 calories; protein 0.2g; carbohydrates 18.2g 6% DV; fat 0.1g; cholesterolmg; sodium 131mg 5% DV.

# Delicious Beef Tongue Tacos

**Prep:** 15 mins **Cook:** 8 hrs 15 mins **Total:** 8 hrs 30 mins **Servings:** 20 **Yield:** 20 tacos

**Ingredients**

- 1 beef tongue
- ½ white onion, sliced
- 5 cloves garlic, crushed
- 1 bay leaf
- 1 pinch salt to taste
- 3 tablespoons vegetable oil

- 5 plum tomato (blank)s Roma tomatoes
- 5 peppers serrano peppers
- 1 pinch salt to taste
- ½ onion, diced
- 2 (10 ounce) packages corn tortillas

**Directions**

**Step 1**

Place the beef tongue in a slow cooker and cover with water. Add the onion slices, garlic, and bay leaf. Season with salt. Cover and cook on Low overnight or 8 hours. Remove the tongue and shred the meat into strands.

**Step 2**

Heat the oil in a skillet over medium heat. Cook the tomatoes and peppers in the hot oil until softened on all sides. Remove the tomatoes and peppers in a blender, keeping the oil on the heat; season with salt. Blend briefly until still slightly chunky. Cook the diced onion in the skillet until translucent; stir in the tomato mixture. Cook another 5 to 6 minutes. Build the tacos by placing shredded tongue meat into a tortilla and spooning salsa over the meat.

**Nutrition Facts**

**Per Serving:**

226.7 calories; protein 11.4g 23% DV; carbohydrates 14g 5% DV; fat 14g 22% DV; cholesterol 65.5mg 22% DV; sodium 46.2mg 2% DV.

# Jamaican Jerk Sauce

**Prep:** 15 mins **Total:** 15 mins **Servings:** 4 **Yield:** 4 servings

## Ingredients

- 1 bunch green onions, chopped
- ½ cup peanut oil
- ½ cup vinegar
- 3 tablespoons ground allspice
- 3 peppers habanero peppers
- 1 (1 inch) piece fresh ginger, peeled
- 5 cloves garlic, peeled
- 2 lime (2" dia)s limes, juiced
- ¼ cup dark brown sugar
- 2 tablespoons chopped fresh thyme
- 2 tablespoons soy sauce
- 2 tablespoons ketchup
- 1 tablespoon whole black peppercorns
- 1 tablespoon ground cinnamon

## Directions

**Step 1**

Blend green onions, peanut oil, vinegar, allspice, habanero peppers, ginger, garlic, lime juice, brown sugar, thyme, soy sauce, ketchup, peppercorns, and cinnamon in a blender until smooth.

## Nutrition Facts

**Per Serving:**

354.5 calories; protein 2.6g 5% DV; carbohydrates 29.2g 9% DV; fat 27.7g 43% DV; cholesterolmg; sodium 553.3mg 22% DV.

# Pina Colada Cocktail

**Prep:** 5 mins **Total:** 5 mins **Servings:** 1 **Yield:** 1 cocktail

## Ingredients

- 3 fluid ounces light rum
- 3 tablespoons cream of coconut
- 3 tablespoons crushed pineapple
- 2 cups ice

**Directions**

**Step 1**

Combine rum, cream of coconut, pineapple, and ice in a blender. Puree on high speed until smooth. Pour into chilled Collins glass and serve with a straw.

**Nutrition Facts**

**Per Serving:**

423.1 calories; protein 0.9g 2% DV; carbohydrates 37.4g 12% DV; fat 9.3g 14% DV; cholesterolmg; sodium 21.8mg 1% DV.

# Quick Cantaloupe Juice

**Prep:** 10 mins **Total:** 10 mins **Servings:** 2 **Yield:** 2 servings

**Ingredients**

- ½ cantaloupe - peeled, seeded, and cubed
- ¾ cup milk
- 1 tablespoon white sugar

**Directions**

**Step 1**

Place cantaloupe in a blender and top with milk and sugar. Cover and blend until smooth.

**Nutrition Facts**

**Per Serving:**

116.9 calories; protein 4.2g 8% DV; carbohydrates 21.8g 7% DV; fat 2.1g 3% DV; cholesterol 7.3mg 2% DV; sodium 59.6mg 2% DV.

# Dry Buttermilk Ranch Mix

**Prep:** 10 mins **Total:** 10 mins **Servings:** 20 **Yield:** 20 servings

**Ingredients**

- ¼ cup dry buttermilk powder
- 2 tablespoons dried minced onion
- 2 tablespoons dried parsley
- 1 tablespoon dried chives
- ¼ teaspoon salt, or to taste
- 1 teaspoon garlic powder
- 1 teaspoon dried celery flakes
- ½ teaspoon white pepper
- ¼ teaspoon paprika
- ¼ teaspoon dried dill weed

**Directions**

**Step 1**

Mix the buttermilk powder, dried onion, parsley, chives, salt, garlic powder, dried celery flakes, white pepper, paprika, and dill together, and store in a cool, dry place. For a finer texture, place ingredients in a blender and pulse several times.

**Cook's Note**

These ingredients are easy to play around with. If you like more salt, add more. I love garlic, but this amount might be too overpowering for some. I also like to add cayenne when I'm looking for a kick.

**Nutrition Facts**

**Per Serving:**

8.5 calories; protein 0.6g 1% DV; carbohydrates 1.3g; fat 0.1g; cholesterol 1mg; sodium 39mg 2% DV.

# Creamy Banana Strawberry Split Smoothie

**Prep:** 10 mins **Total:** 10 mins **Servings:** 4 **Yield:** 4 servings

**Ingredients**

- 1 cup almond milk
- 1 chopped banana, frozen
- ¾ cup strawberries
- 3 eaches ice cubes
- 1 scoop vanilla protein powder
- 1 teaspoon vanilla extract
- 1 teaspoon honey
- 1 teaspoon ground flax seed
- 1 teaspoon ground chia seeds
- ½ teaspoon ground cinnamon

**Directions**

**Step 1**

Blend almond milk, banana, strawberries, ice cubes, protein powder, vanilla extract, honey, ground flax seeds, ground chia seeds, and cinnamon in a blender until smooth.

**Nutrition Facts**

**Per Serving:**

111.2 calories; protein 10.4g 21% DV; carbohydrates 14.4g 5% DV; fat 1.6g 3% DV; cholesterol 3.1mg 1% DV; sodium 94.7mg 4% DV.

# ABC Pudding - Avocado, Banana, Chocolate Delight

**Prep:** 10 mins **Additional:** 1 hr **Total:** 1 hr 10 mins **Servings:** 6 **Yield:** 6 servings

**Ingredients**

- 1 ripe avocado, peeled and pitted
- 4 medium (7" to 7-7/8" long)s very ripe bananas
- ¼ cup unsweetened cocoa powder, plus more for garnish

**Directions**

**Step 1**

Place avocados, bananas, and cocoa powder in a blender; puree until smooth.

**Step 2**

Pour pudding into serving bowls and sprinkle additional cocoa powder on top for garnish.

**Step 3**

Chill in refrigerator for texture and flavor to develop, at least 1 hour.

**Cook's note:**

For a colder treat, use frozen banana slices instead. After pureed, place your pudding in the freezer for 5 minutes before serving.

**Nutrition Facts**

**Per Serving:**

131.8 calories; protein 2.2g 5% DV; carbohydrates 22.8g 7% DV; fat 5.7g 9% DV; cholesterolmg; sodium 3.9mg.

# Mango-Peach Smoothie

**Prep:** 10 mins **Total:** 10 mins **Servings:** 2 **Yield:** 2 smoothies

**Ingredients**

- 1 peach, sliced
- 1 mango, peeled and diced
- ½ cup vanilla soy milk
- ½ cup orange juice, or as needed

**Directions**

**Step 1**

Place the peach, mango, soy milk, and orange juice into a blender. Cover, and puree until smooth. Pour into glasses to serve.

**Nutrition Facts**

**Per Serving:**
104.8 calories; protein 2.5g 5% DV; carbohydrates 22.3g 7% DV; fat 1.3g 2% DV; cholesterolmg; sodium 29mg 1% DV.

# Fresh Grapefruit Juice Smoothie

**Prep:** 15 mins **Total:** 15 mins **Servings:** 2 **Yield:** 2 servings

**Ingredients**

- 1 ⅓ cups fresh red grapefruit juice
- 8 large strawberries
- 2 medium bananas, sliced
- 1 (8 ounce) container strawberry-banana yogurt
- 2 tablespoons honey
- 1 cup crushed ice

**Directions**

**Step 1**

Place the grapefruit juice, strawberries, bananas, yogurt, honey, and ice into a blender. Cover, and blend until smooth.

**Nutrition Facts**

**Per Serving:**

361.2 calories; protein 7.2g 14% DV; carbohydrates 85g 27% DV; fat 1.8g 3% DV; cholesterol 5mg 2% DV; sodium 74.4mg 3% DV.

# Breakfast Banana Green Smoothie

**Prep:** 5 mins **Total:** 5 mins **Servings:** 1 **Yield:** 1 serving

## Ingredients

- 2 cups baby spinach leaves, or to taste
- 1 banana
- 1 carrot, peeled and cut into large chunks
- ¾ cup plain fat-free Greek yogurt, or to taste
- ¾ cup ice
- 2 tablespoons honey

## Directions

### Step 1

Put spinach, banana, carrot, yogurt, ice, and honey in a blender; blend until smooth.

## Nutrition Facts

**Per Serving:**

366.8 calories; protein 18.6g 37% DV; carbohydrates 77.4g 25% DV; fat 0.8g 1% DV; cholesterolmg; sodium 162.4mg 7% DV.

# Honey Balsamic Vinaigrette

**Prep:** 15 mins **Total:** 15 mins **Servings:** 12 **Yield:** 1 1/2 cups

## Ingredients

- ½ cup balsamic vinegar
- 1 small onion, chopped
- 1 tablespoon soy sauce
- 3 tablespoons honey
- 1 tablespoon white sugar
- 2 cloves garlic, minced
- ½ teaspoon crushed red pepper flakes
- ⅔ cup extra-virgin olive oil

**Directions**

**Step 1**

Place the vinegar, onion, soy sauce, honey, sugar, garlic, and red pepper flakes into a blender. Puree on high, gradually adding the olive oil. Continue pureeing 2 minutes, or until thick.

**Nutrition Facts**

**Per Serving:**

142.7 calories; protein 0.2g 1% DV; carbohydrates 7.8g 3% DV; fat 12.5g 19% DV; cholesterolmg; sodium 78.3mg 3% DV.

# Peruvian Aji-Style Sauce

**Prep:** 15 mins **Total:** 15 mins **Servings:** 10 **Yield:** 10 servings

**Ingredients**

- 1 head romaine lettuce, stem-end trimmed and discarded
- ½ bunch fresh cilantro, stems removed
- 5 eaches green onions
- ¼ cup mayonnaise
- 2 medium (blank)s jalapeno peppers, seeded
- 1 clove garlic
- 1 pinch salt and ground black pepper to taste

**Directions**

**Step 1**

Place romaine lettuce, cilantro, green onions, mayonnaise, jalapeno peppers, garlic, salt, and black pepper into a blender; blend until smooth, about 2 minutes.

**Nutrition Facts**

**Per Serving:**

49.5 calories; protein 0.7g 1% DV; carbohydrates 2.2g 1% DV; fat 4.5g 7% DV; cholesterol 2.1mg 1% DV; sodium 36.5mg 2% DV.

# Watermelon Lime Agua Fresca

**Prep:** 15 mins **Additional:** 1 hr **Total:** 1 hr 15 mins **Servings:** 10 **Yield:** 2 1/2 quarts

## Ingredients

- 8 cups water, divided
- 5 cups peeled, cubed, and seeded watermelon
- ½ cup white sugar, or more to taste
- ⅓ cup lime juice, or more to taste

## Directions

### Step 1

Combine 1 cup water, watermelon, and sugar in a blender; process until smooth. Pour into a large pitcher; stir in lime juice and remaining 7 cups water. Taste;  sugar or lime juice. Refrigerate until chilled, about 1 hour.

## Nutrition Facts

**Per Serving:**

63.6 calories; protein 0.5g 1% DV; carbohydrates 16.4g 5% DV; fat 0.1g; cholesterolmg; sodium 6.6mg.

# Blueberry Banana Milkshake

**Prep:** 10 mins **Total:** 10 mins  **Servings:** 4 **Yield:** 4 servings

## Ingredients

- 2 cups vanilla ice cream
- 1 cup milk
- 1 ½ cups blueberries
- 1 banana
- ¼ cup white sugar
- 1 teaspoon vanilla extract

## Directions

### Step 1

Place vanilla ice cream and milk in a blender and blend until smooth. Add blueberries, banana, sugar, and vanilla extract; blend until evenly mixed.

## Nutrition Facts

**Per Serving:**

271.9 calories; protein 5g 10% DV; carbohydrates 45.7g 15% DV; fat 8.7g 13% DV; cholesterol 33.9mg 11% DV; sodium 78.7mg 3% DV.

# Summertime Mango Drink

**Prep:** 5 mins **Total:** 5 mins **Servings:** 4 **Yield:** 4 servings

**Ingredients**

- 2 eaches mangoes, cut into cubes
- 1 cup ice cubes
- 1 teaspoon vanilla extract
- 1 tablespoon white sugar
- 1 ⅔ cups milk

**Directions**

**Step 1**

Combine mangoes, ice cubes, vanilla extract, and sugar in a blender; pour in milk. Blend until liquefied.

**Nutrition Facts**

**Per Serving:**

114.8 calories; protein 3.7g 8% DV; carbohydrates 20.8g 7% DV; fat 2.2g 3% DV; cholesterol 8.1mg 3% DV; sodium 43.3mg 2% DV.

# Pear Vinaigrette

**Prep:** 10 mins **Total:** 10 mins **Servings:** 12 **Yield:** 1 1/2 cups

**Ingredients**

- 1 ripe pear - peeled, cored, and chopped
- ½ cup white wine
- 1 clove garlic, chopped
- 2 teaspoons Dijon mustard
- ¼ cup white balsamic vinegar
- 1 teaspoon ground black pepper
- ¼ teaspoon sea salt
- ½ cup olive oil

**Directions**

**Step 1**

Blend the pear, white wine, garlic, Dijon mustard, white balsamic vinegar, black pepper, and sea salt in a blender until well combined; drizzle the olive oil into the mixture in a thin, steady stream while continuing to blend. Blend a few seconds longer until the salad dressing is thick and creamy.

**Nutrition Facts**

**Per Serving:**

101.1 calories; protein 0.1g; carbohydrates 3.6g 1% DV; fat 9g 14% DV; cholesterolmg; sodium 59.7mg 2% DV.

# Boba (Coconut Milk Black Tea with Tapioca Pearls)

**Prep:** 10 mins **Cook:** 55 mins **Additional:** 1 hr 5 mins **Total:** 2 hrs 10 mins **Servings:** 5

**Yield:** 5 glasses

**Ingredients**

**Tapioca Pearls:**

- 7 cups cold water
- ½ (8.8 ounce) package tapioca starch balls
- ½ cup brown sugar
- ½ cup white sugar

**Tea:**

- 4 cups brewed black tea (such as Lipton), chilled
- 1 (14 ounce) can coconut cream
- 12 ice cubes ice cubes
- 1 cup milk
- ⅔ cup white sugar

**Directions**

**Step 1**

Bring water to a boil in a large stockpot. Pour in tapioca and simmer for 25 minutes. Stir occasionally to prevent sticking. Remove from heat and let balls sit in water for 25 minutes.

**Step 2**

Return stockpot to the heat; simmer and stir for 25 minutes more. Remove from heat and let rest again until centers of the balls are no longer powder, another 25 minutes. Drain.

**Step 3**

Combine brown sugar and white sugar in a large bowl. Pour tapioca balls into the sugar mixture. Cover with a damp cloth and let rest for 15 minutes while preparing the tea.

**Step 4**

Process tea, coconut cream, ice, milk, and sugar together in a blender until combined.

**Step 5**

Scoop 1/4 cup of the tapioca into each tall glass and fill with tea. Enjoy with large straws to suck up the tapioca, or use spoons.

**Cook's Notes:**

For a more pronounced black tea taste, use Hong Kong-style tea bags.

Substitute half-and-half for the milk if desired.

**Nutrition Facts**

**Per Serving:**
641.9 calories; protein 4.6g 9% DV; carbohydrates 98.5g 32% DV; fat 28.5g 44% DV; cholesterol 3.9mg 1% DV; sodium 46.7mg 2% DV.

# Middle Eastern Garlic Sauce

**Prep:** 10 mins **Cook:** 15 mins **Total:** 25 mins **Servings:** 10 **Yield:** 10 servings

**Ingredients**

- 3 small russet potatoes, peeled
- 1 head garlic, peeled and crushed
- 1 ½ teaspoons salt
- ⅓ cup lemon juice
- ½ cup canola oil

**Directions**

**Step 1**

Place potatoes into a large pot and cover with salted water; bring to a boil. Reduce heat to medium-low and simmer until tender, 15 to 20 minutes. Drain and transfer to a bowl; mash until smooth. Set aside to cool.

**Step 2**

Put garlic, salt, and lemon juice in a blender or food processor; pour in enough oil to lightly coat garlic cloves. Blend mixture on high; slowly stream remaining oil through the top opening of the blender or food processor until mixture is smooth. Add mashed potatoes, about 2 to 3 tablespoons at a time, to the garlic mixture while blender is still running. Continue adding potatoes until all are incorporated. Transfer sauce to a bowl and refrigerate until chilled, 1 hour to overnight.

**Nutrition Facts**

**Per Serving:**

148.7 calories; protein 1.4g 3% DV; carbohydrates 11.5g 4% DV; fat 11.3g 17% DV; cholesterolmg; sodium 352.9mg 14% DV.

# Cliff's Hot Sauce

**Prep:** 10 mins **Total:** 10 mins **Servings:** 16 **Yield:** 1 quart

**Ingredients**

- 2 medium (blank)s jalapeno peppers
- 1 (28 ounce) can whole tomatoes in juice
- 1 slice white onion
- 1 teaspoon minced garlic
- ½ teaspoon ground cumin
- ¼ teaspoon dried oregano
- ¼ teaspoon salt

**Directions**

**Step 1**

Remove the stems from the jalapeno peppers, and the seeds from one jalapeno. Place both jalapeno peppers, tomatoes with liquid, onion, garlic, cumin, oregano, and salt in a blender; pulse to desired consistency. Serve

**Nutrition Facts**

**Per Serving:**

9.8 calories; protein 0.4g 1% DV; carbohydrates 2.2g 1% DV; fat 0.1g; cholesterolmg; sodium 106.6mg 4% DV.

# Strawberry Banana Smoothie

**Prep:** 5 mins **Total:** 5 mins **Servings:** 2 **Yield:** 3 cups

## Ingredients

- 1 ½ cups vanilla yogurt
- 2 medium (7" to 7-7/8" long)s bananas, cut up
- ½ cup frozen strawberries
- 2 tablespoons wheat germ
- 1 tablespoon honey

## Directions

### Step 1

Combine the yogurt, bananas, strawberries, wheat germ, and honey in a blender; blend until smooth, about 1 minute.

## Nutrition Facts

**Per Serving:**

331.7 calories; protein 12.2g 24% DV; carbohydrates 68g 22% DV; fat 3.4g 5% DV; cholesterol 9.2mg 3% DV; sodium 124.5mg 5% DV.

# Sweet Pork for Burritos

**Prep:** 30 mins **Cook:** 8 hrs **Total:** 8 hrs 30 mins **Servings:** 12 **Yield:** 12 servings

## Ingredients

- 3 pounds pork shoulder roast
- 2 cups salsa
- 1 (12 fluid ounce) can or bottle cola-flavored carbonated beverage
- 2 cups brown sugar
- ½ (1.27 ounce) packet fajita seasoning
- 2 tablespoons taco seasoning mix
- 1 (7 ounce) can chopped green chilies

## Directions

### Step 1

Place pork roast in the crock of a slow cooker, and add 4 cups water. Cook on High for 5 hours.

**Step 2**

Remove pork from the slow cooker and drain liquid. Cut the pork into 4 pieces, and set aside. Puree salsa in blender. Combine the pureed salsa, cola, brown sugar, fajita seasoning, taco seasoning, and green chilies in the crock of the slow cooker. Add the pork, and cook on High for an additional 3 hours.

**Step 3**

Remove the pork, and shred with 2 forks. Serve.

**Nutrition Facts**

**Per Serving:**

355.1 calories; protein 23g 46% DV; carbohydrates 32.6g 11% DV; fat 14.7g 23% DV; cholesterol 72.6mg 24% DV; sodium 727.8mg 29% DV.

# No Cook Applesauce

**Prep:** 15 mins **Total:** 15 mins **Servings:** 16 **Yield:** 16 servings

**Ingredients**

- 12 medium (2-3/4" dia) (approx 3 per lb)s apples - peeled, cored, and chopped
- 1 cup brown sugar
- 1 cup water
- 1 ½ tablespoons lemon juice
- 1 teaspoon ground cinnamon

**Directions**

**Step 1**

Blend apples, brown sugar, water, lemon juice, and cinnamon in a blender until smooth.

**Nutrition Facts**

**Per Serving:**

106.8 calories; protein 0.3g 1% DV; carbohydrates 28g 9% DV; fat 0.2g; cholesterolmg; sodium 5.4mg.

# Simple Summer Smoothie

**Prep:** 10 mins **Total:** 10 mins **Servings:** 4 **Yield:** 4 cups

**Ingredients**

- 1 banana
- 1 cup frozen strawberries
- 1 cup frozen blueberries
- 1 cup frozen cherries
- 4 ice cubes ice cubes
- ½ cup orange juice
- ¾ cup vanilla yogurt
- ½ teaspoon honey

**Directions**

**Step 1**

Place the banana, strawberries, blueberries, cherries, and ice cubes into a blender. Pour in the orange juice, vanilla yogurt, and honey. Puree until smooth.

**Nutrition Facts**

**Per Serving:**

139 calories; protein 3.6g 7% DV; carbohydrates 31.1g 10% DV; fat 1.2g 2% DV; cholesterol 2.3mg 1% DV; sodium 33.5mg 1% DV.

# Keto Avocado-Spinach Smoothie

**Prep:** 5 mins **Total:** 5 mins **Servings:** 2 **Yield:** 2 servings

**Ingredients**

- ½ cup coconut milk
- ½ cup water, or more as needed
- 3 eaches ice cubes
- ½ medium avocado, pitted and scooped from shell
- ½ cup fresh spinach
- 2 tablespoons erythritol
- 1 tablespoon medium-chain triglyceride (MCT) oil
- ½ teaspoon vanilla powder

**Directions**

**Step 1**

Combine coconut milk, water, ice cubes, avocado, spinach, erythritol, MCT oil, and vanilla powder in a blender. Blend until smooth.

**Cook's Notes:**

Feel free to replace coconut milk with 1/4 cup heavy whipping cream plus 1/4 cup water.

You can substitute extra-virgin coconut oil for the MCT oil.

Substitute 1 teaspoon vanilla extract for the vanilla powder if desired, and 5 to 8 drops of stevia extract instead of erythritol.

Optional add-ins: 1/4 cup chocolate, vanilla, or plain whey protein, egg white protein powder (such as Jay Robb (R)), collagen powder, or plant-based NuZest(R).

**Nutrition Facts**

**Per Serving:**

255.6 calories; protein 2.4g 5% DV; carbohydrates 17.6g 6% DV; fat 26.4g 41% DV; cholesterolmg; sodium 19.5mg 1% DV.

# Daiquiri

**Servings:** 2 **Yield:** 2 drinks

## Ingredients

- 1 (6 ounce) can frozen lemonade concentrate
- 6 fluid ounces chilled lemon-lime soda
- 6 fluid ounces light rum
- ½ (10 ounce) package frozen sliced strawberries
- 2 cups ice cubes

## Directions

**Step 1**

In the container of a blender, combine the lemonade concentrate, lemon-lime soda, rum and strawberries. Cover, and blend until smooth. Add ice and blend to desired thickness.

**Nutrition Facts**

**Per Serving:**

452.2 calories; protein 0.6g 1% DV; carbohydrates 67.4g 22% DV; fat 0.3g; cholesterolmg; sodium 23.3mg 1% DV.

# Orange Creamsicle Protein Shake

**Prep:** 5 mins **Total:** 5 mins **Servings:** 1 **Yield:** 1 shake

**Ingredients**

- 1 orange, zested and peeled
- 1 cup soy milk
- 1 (5.3 ounce) container plain Greek yogurt
- 1 scoop vanilla protein powder
- 5 eaches ice cubes
- 1 teaspoon vanilla extract

**Directions**

**Step 1**

Combine orange segments, zest, soy milk, yogurt, protein powder, ice, and vanilla extract in a blender. Blend until smooth.

**Cook's Notes:**

Substitute vanilla Greek yogurt for the plain yogurt if desired.

For a more intense orange flavor, freeze orange juice and use in place of ice cubes.

**Nutrition Facts**

**Per Serving:**

510.4 calories; protein 54.1g 108% DV; carbohydrates 26.8g 9% DV; fat 19.8g 31% DV; cholesterol 44.7mg 15% DV; sodium 433.1mg 17% DV.

# Blender Bearnaise Sauce

**Prep:** 10 mins **Cook:** 5 mins **Total:** 15 mins **Servings:** 8 **Yield:** 8 servings

**Ingredients**

- 2 tablespoons white wine
- 1 tablespoon cider vinegar
- 1 teaspoon dried tarragon
- ½ teaspoon dried minced onion
- ¼ teaspoon ground black pepper
- ½ cup butter

- 3 large egg yolks egg yolks
- 2 tablespoons lemon juice
- ½ teaspoon salt
- 1 pinch cayenne pepper

## Directions

### Step 1

Combine wine, vinegar, tarragon, onion, and black pepper in a skillet; bring to a boil and cook until almost all the liquid is evaporated, 2 to 3 minutes.

### Step 2

Place butter in a microwave-safe bowl and heat in microwave until fully melted, 30 seconds to 1 minute.

### Step 3

Place tarragon mixture, egg yolks, lemon juice, salt, and cayenne pepper in a blender; pulse until combined, 5 to 10 seconds. Remove the small hole cover from lid; stream butter into egg mixture while blender is running until sauce is completely blended and smooth.

## Nutrition Facts

### Per Serving:

127.2 calories; protein 1.2g 2% DV; carbohydrates 0.9g; fat 13.2g 20% DV; cholesterol 107.3mg 36% DV; sodium 230.6mg 9% DV.

# Orange Milkshake

**Prep:** 5 mins **Total:** 5 mins **Servings:** 1 **Yield:** 1 milkshake

## Ingredients

- 1 ½ cups orange juice
- 2 scoops vanilla ice cream
- ½ cup milk
- 2 teaspoons white sugar

## Directions

### Step 1

Combine orange juice, ice cream, milk, and sugar in a blender; blend until smooth. Pour milkshake into a glass.

**Nutrition Facts**

**Per Serving:**

345.1 calories; protein 8.1g 16% DV; carbohydrates 62.6g 20% DV; fat 7.8g 12% DV; cholesterol 28.2mg 9% DV; sodium 87.3mg 4% DV.

# Licuado de Mango

**Prep:** 10 mins **Total:** 10 mins **Servings:** 2 **Yield:** 2 cups

## Ingredients

- 1 mango - peeled, seeded and diced
- 1 ½ cups milk
- 3 tablespoons honey
- 1 cup ice cubes

## Directions

### Step 1

Place the mango, milk, honey and ice cubes into a blender. Cover and blend until smooth. Serve immediately.

**Nutrition Facts**

**Per Serving:**

254.5 calories; protein 6.7g 13% DV; carbohydrates 52.1g 17% DV; fat 3.9g 6% DV; cholesterol 14.6mg 5% DV; sodium 78.4mg 3% DV.

# Blended Mocha Drink

**Prep:** 10 mins **Total:** 10 mins **Servings:** 2 **Yield:** 2 servings

## Ingredients

- ¾ cup brewed espresso
- ¼ cup sweetened condensed milk
- 1 cup whole milk
- 10 eaches ice cubes, or as needed
- 3 tablespoons chocolate syrup, or more to taste

## Directions

### Step 1

Stir espresso and sweetened condensed milk together in a bowl. Add milk and stir; pour into a blender. Add ice and chocolate syrup to the espresso mixture. Blend until smooth.

**Nutrition Facts**

**Per Serving:**

276.5 calories; protein 7.7g 15% DV; carbohydrates 44.7g 14% DV; fat 7.8g 12% DV; cholesterol 25.2mg 8% DV; sodium 133.4mg 5% DV.

# Authentic Mexican Restaurant Style Salsa

**Prep:** 5 mins **Additional:** 8 hrs **Total:** 8 hrs 5 mins **Servings:** 14 **Yield:** 3 1/2 cups

**Ingredients**

- 1 (28 ounce) can crushed tomatoes
- 10 slices pickled jalapeno peppers with juice, or to taste
- 10 eaches cilantro leaves
- ½ teaspoon salt
- ¼ teaspoon garlic powder

**Directions**

**Step 1**

Blend crushed tomatoes, jalapeno peppers with juice, cilantro leaves, salt, and garlic powder in a blender until smooth. Refrigerate 8 hours to overnight.

**Nutrition Facts**

**Per Serving:**

19 calories; protein 1g 2% DV; carbohydrates 4.3g 1% DV; fat 0.2g; cholesterolmg; sodium 205.1mg 8% DV.

# Dragon Fruit Colada

**Prep:** 10 mins **Total:** 10 mins **Servings:** 2 **Yield:** 2 drinks

**Ingredients**

- 1 cup ice cubes
- ½ dragon fruit

- ½ cup cream of coconut
- ½ cup rum
- ¼ cup coconut milk
- ¼ cup pineapple chunks

**Directions**

**Step 1**

Fill a blender halfway with ice cubes. Scoop out flesh from dragon fruit half and place in the blender. Add cream of coconut, rum, coconut milk, and pineapple chunks; puree until smooth. Pour into 2 glasses.

**Cook's Note:**

When selecting a dragon fruit, feel the stem. It should bend without breaking when you touch it. If it is brittle, move on. The fruit should feel slightly spongy, almost like a kiwi. If it is very firm, leave it for a day or two and check again. The skin should be a bright pink color. Chilling it brings out the flavor.

**Nutrition Facts**

**Per Serving:**
502.8 calories; protein 0.9g 2% DV; carbohydrates 53.8g 17% DV; fat 19.4g 30% DV; cholesterolmg; sodium 47.3mg 2% DV.

# Frozen Caramel Latte

**Prep:** 10 mins **Total:** 10 mins **Servings:** 1 **Yield:** 1 serving

**Ingredients**

- 3 fluid ounces brewed espresso
- 1 tablespoon caramel sauce
- 2 tablespoons white sugar
- ¾ cup milk
- 1 ½ cups ice cubes
- 2 tablespoons whipped cream

**Directions**

**Step 1**

Place the espresso, caramel sauce, and sugar into a blender pitcher. Blend on high until the caramel and sugar dissolve into the espresso. Pour in the milk and add the ice; continue blending until smooth and frothy. Top with whipped cream to serve.

**Nutrition Facts**

**Per Serving:**

293.4 calories; protein 6.8g 14% DV; carbohydrates 47.5g 15% DV; fat 9.3g 14% DV; cholesterol 35.4mg 12% DV; sodium 164.1mg 7% DV.

# Almond Milk Frappuccino

**Prep:** 5 mins **Total:** 5 mins **Servings:** 1 **Yield:** 1 drink

## Ingredients

- 1 cup ice
- 1 cup vanilla-flavored almond milk
- 2 shots brewed espresso, chilled
- 1 teaspoon honey, or to taste

## Directions

**Step 1**

Blend ice, almond milk, espresso, and honey in a blender until smooth.

**Cook's Note:**

Any sweetener can be used in place of the honey.

**Nutrition Facts**

**Per Serving:**

120.4 calories; protein 1.2g 2% DV; carbohydrates 23.3g 8% DV; fat 2.8g 4% DV; cholesterolmg; sodium 176.6mg 7% DV.

# World's Easiest Refreshing Smoothie

**Prep:** 10 mins **Total:** 10 mins **Servings:** 1 **Yield:** 1 serving

## Ingredients

- ½ (16 ounce) can pineapple chunks, undrained
- 5 berry (blank)s frozen strawberries

## Directions

**Step 1**

Blend pineapple, reserved pineapple juice, and strawberries together in a blender until smooth.

**Nutrition Facts**

**Per Serving:**

154.6 calories; protein 1.2g 2% DV; carbohydrates 40.4g 13% DV; fat 0.2g; cholesterolmg; sodium 3.3mg.

# Coconut Oil Coffee

**Prep:** 5 mins **Total:** 5 mins **Servings:** 2 **Yield:** 2 servings

**Ingredients**

- 2 cups hot coffee
- 2 tablespoons coconut oil
- 2 tablespoons unsalted butter

**Directions**

**Step 1**

Blend coffee, coconut oil, and butter together in a blender until oil and butter are melted and coffee is frothy.

**Tips**

**Cook's Notes:**

Use unsalted grass-fed butter. Preheat your blender with hot water to make sure your coffee doesn't start out cold.

**Nutrition Facts**

**Per Serving:**

224.2 calories; protein 0.4g 1% DV; carbohydratesg; fat 25.6g 39% DV; cholesterol 30.5mg 10% DV; sodium 6.3mg.

# Banana Lassi

**Prep:** 10 mins **Total:** 10 mins **Servings:** 2 **Yield:** 2 servings

**Ingredients**

- 2 eaches over-ripe bananas, broken
  into chunks
- 1 ¼ cups thick plain yogurt
- ⅓ cup milk, or more to taste
- 2 ice cubes ice cubes
- 2 tablespoons white sugar

**Directions**

**Step 1**

Blend bananas, yogurt, milk, ice cubes, and sugar together in a blender until smooth.

**Cook's Notes:**

The servings are small in comparison to restaurants outside of India, but I think it's probably a good idea to consume smaller amounts of good active bacteria in yogurt.

Substitute honey for sugar, if desired.

Use good strong-flavored yogurt: it makes all the difference. Milk is just to get things moving, so you can adjust to preferred taste/texture.

**Nutrition Facts**

**Per Serving:**

270.2 calories; protein 10.7g 21% DV; carbohydrates 52.1g 17% DV; fat 3.6g 6% DV; cholesterol 12.4mg 4% DV; sodium 125.7mg 5% DV.

# Superfood Berry-Green Smoothie

**Prep:** 10 mins **Total:** 10 mins **Servings:** 1 **Yield:** 1 smoothie

**Ingredients**

- 1 ¼ cups unsweetened almond milk
- 1 clementine (such as Cuties),
  peeled
- ½ cup frozen raspberries
- 1 cup spinach, or more to taste
- 1 tablespoon chia seeds
- 1 tablespoon flaxseed meal
- 1 cup frozen blueberries
- 1 scoop vanilla protein powder

**Directions**

**Step 1**

Place almond milk, clementine, raspberries, spinach, chia seeds, flaxseed meal, blueberries, and protein powder in the blender, respectively. Blend on high until smooth, about 30 seconds.

**Cook's Notes:**

Substitute kale for the spinach if desired.

If using fresh, not frozen fruit, you may need to add a few ice cubes in order to thicken the smoothie up.

**Nutrition Facts**

**Per Serving:**

489.7 calories; protein 44g 88% DV; carbohydrates 58g 19% DV; fat 11.5g 18% DV; cholesterol 12.5mg 4% DV; sodium 442.8mg 18% DV.

# Berries and Cream Smoothie

**Prep:** 5 mins **Total:** 5 mins **Servings:** 3 **Yield:** 3 servings

**Ingredients**

- 1 cup heavy cream
- ¾ cup half-and-half
- ¼ cup white sugar
- ½ teaspoon vanilla extract
- 1 cup frozen blueberries
- 1 cup frozen strawberries
- ½ cup frozen raspberries
- ½ cup frozen blackberries
- ½ cup milk

**Directions**

**Step 1**

Pour cream and half-and-half into an electric blender and blend on low speed until it begins to thicken. Add sugar and vanilla extract and mix for about 30 seconds. Add blueberries, strawberries, raspberries, and blackberries. Blend until smooth, adding milk if necessary to make blending easier.

**Cook's Notes:**

If you choose to use fresh fruits instead of frozen, then you can simply add 1 to 2 cups of ice and omit the last 1/2 cup milk.

The 3/4 cup half-and-half may be substituted with regular milk (though it won't be quite as thick and creamy).

**Nutrition Facts**

**Per Serving:**

516.7 calories; protein 5.9g 12% DV; carbohydrates 42.4g 14% DV; fat 37.6g 58% DV; cholesterol 134.3mg 45% DV; sodium 74.2mg 3% DV.

# Kale Orange Banana Smoothie

**Prep:** 10 mins **Total:** 10 mins **Servings:** 1 **Yield:** 1 serving

## Ingredients

- 1 orange, peeled
- ½ cup water
- 1 leaf kale, torn into several pieces
- 2 eaches ripe bananas, peeled

## Directions

**Step 1**

Blend the orange in a blender until mostly juice.

**Step 2**

Add the water and kale; blend again on High speed until kale is liquefied.

**Step 3**

Break the bananas into chunks and add to the blender. Start blending on a lower speed until the banana is incorporated. Increase speed to blend the mixture into a pudding-like texture.

**Nutrition Facts**

**Per Serving:**

220 calories; protein 3.2g 7% DV; carbohydrates 55.9g 18% DV; fat 0.9g 1% DV; cholesterolmg; sodium 14.5mg 1% DV.

# Bulletproof Hot Chocolate

Prep: 5 mins Total: 5 mins Servings: 1 Yield: 1 serving

## Ingredients

- 11 fluid ounces hot water
- 2 tablespoons unsalted butter
- 1 tablespoon medium-chain triglyceride (MCT) oil
- 1 tablespoon cacao powder
- 1 tablespoon cacao butter
- ⅛ teaspoon vanilla powder
- 6 drops liquid stevia, or to taste
- 1 pinch salt

## Directions

### Step 1

Combine hot water, butter, MCT oil, cacao powder, cacao butter, vanilla powder, liquid stevia, and salt in a blender; blend until smooth.

### Cook's Notes:

You can add 1 tablespoon hydrolyzed collagen protein powder and vitamin/supplement powders to the hot chocolate if desired.

I use grass-fed butter. Ghee can also be used in place of the butter, if desired.

## Nutrition Facts

**Per Serving:**

477.6 calories; protein 3.1g 6% DV; carbohydrates 9g 3% DV; fat 50g 77% DV; cholesterol 61.1mg 20% DV; sodium 172.1mg 7% DV.

# Quick Avocado Smoothie

Prep: 10 mins Total: 10 mins Servings: 1 Yield: 1 smoothie

## Ingredients

- 1 ¼ cups almond milk
- 1 avocado - peeled, pitted, and sliced
- 1 small banana, sliced
- ¼ cup ice, or as needed
- 1 tablespoon honey

**Directions**

**Step 1**

Blend almond milk, avocado, banana, ice, and honey in a blender until smooth.

**Nutrition Facts**

**Per Serving:**

555.3 calories; protein 6.5g 13% DV; carbohydrates 68.2g 22% DV; fat 33.1g 51% DV; cholesterolmg; sodium 217.6mg 9% DV.

# Purple Moose - Canadian Smoothie

**Prep:** 10 mins **Total:** 10 mins **Servings:** 2 **Yield:** 2 servings

**Ingredients**

- 15 ice cubes ice cubes
- 1 ripe banana
- ½ cup vanilla rice milk
- ¼ cup fresh blueberries
- 2 tablespoons natural peanut butter
- 2 tablespoons maple syrup

**Directions**

**Step 1**

Combine ice cubes, banana, rice milk, blueberries, peanut butter, and maple syrup in a blender; blend on low speed. Increase speed to medium-high and blend until smooth.

**Cook's Note:**

If necessary, add a bit of rice milk if the ice cubes are bigger and it becomes too thick.

**Nutrition Facts**

**Per Serving:**

240.6 calories; protein 4.9g 10% DV; carbohydrates 39.9g 13% DV; fat 8.7g 13% DV; cholesterolmg; sodium 69.5mg 3% DV.

# Peanut Butter Mango Smoothie

Prep: 5 mins Total: 5 mins Servings: 2 Yield: 2 smoothies

## Ingredients

- 1 cup vanilla yogurt
- 1 banana, broken into chunks
- ½ cup frozen mango chunks
- 2 tablespoons peanut butter, or to taste

## Directions

### Step 1

Blend yogurt, banana, mango, and peanut butter together in a blender until smooth.

## Nutrition Facts

### Per Serving:

279.1 calories; protein 11g 22% DV; carbohydrates 40.6g 13% DV; fat 10g 15% DV; cholesterol 6.1mg 2% DV; sodium 156.9mg 6% DV.

# 3-Minute Mochaccino

Prep: 5 mins Total: 5 mins Servings: 1 Yield: 1 servings

## Ingredients

- ¾ cup milk
- 6 eaches ice cubes
- 1 tablespoon white sugar
- 1 teaspoon instant coffee granules
- 1 teaspoon cocoa powder, or more to taste
- ½ teaspoon vanilla extract, or more to taste
- 1 tablespoon chocolate syrup
- 1 tablespoon whipped cream

## Directions

### Step 1

Blend milk, ice cubes, sugar, instant coffee granules, cocoa powder, and vanilla extract in a blender until smooth.

**Step 2**

Lightly coat the inside of a glass with chocolate syrup. Pour the coffee mixture into the glass. Top with whipped cream to serve.

**Nutrition Facts**

**Per Serving:**

217.6 calories; protein 7g 14% DV; carbohydrates 35.9g 12% DV; fat 5.1g 8% DV; cholesterol 14.6mg 5% DV; sodium 94.2mg 4% DV.

# Watermelon Juice

**Prep:** 5 mins **Total:** 5 mins **Servings:** 4 **Yield:** 4 cups

**Ingredients**

- 2 cups diced seedless watermelon
- 2 cups water
- 1 tablespoon white sugar, or more to taste

**Directions**

**Step 1**

Blend watermelon, water, and sugar in a blender until smooth.

**Nutrition Facts**

**Per Serving:**

34.9 calories; protein 0.5g 1% DV; carbohydrates 8.9g 3% DV; fat 0.1g; cholesterolmg; sodium 4.3mg.

# Refreshing Watermelon Margarita

**Prep:** 10 mins **Additional:** 3 hrs **Total:** 3 hrs 10 mins **Servings:** 2 **Yield:** 2 cocktails

**Ingredients**

- ½ watermelon, cubed
- ¾ cup tequila

- ¼ cup lime juice
- ¼ cup white sugar

**Directions**

**Step 1**

Place watermelon in a blender; blend until smooth. Pour through a fine mesh strainer to remove seeds and pulp.

**Step 2**

Pour watermelon juice into ice cube tray; place in freezer until frozen, about 3 hours.

**Step 3**

Place 4 cups of frozen watermelon cubes, tequila, lime juice, and sugar into a blender; pulse until smooth.

**Nutrition Facts**

**Per Serving:**

403.4 calories; protein 2.2g 4% DV; carbohydrates 53.3g 17% DV; fat 0.5g 1% DV; cholesterolmg; sodium 4.9mg.

# Cream of Asparagus and Mushroom Soup

**Prep:** 15 mins **Cook:** 40 mins **Total:** 55 mins **Servings:** 8 **Yield:** 8 servings

**Ingredients**

- 3 slices bacon
- 1 tablespoon bacon drippings
- ¼ cup butter
- 3 stalks celery, chopped
- 1 onion, diced
- 3 tablespoons all-purpose flour
- 6 cups chicken broth
- 1 potato, peeled and diced
- 1 pound fresh asparagus, tips set aside and stalks chopped
- 1 pinch salt and ground black pepper to taste
- 1 (8 ounce) package sliced fresh mushrooms
- ¾ cup half-and-half cream

**Directions**

**Step 1**

Place the bacon in a large, deep skillet, and cook over medium-high heat, turning occasionally, until evenly browned, about 10 minutes. Drain the bacon slices on a paper towel-lined plate. Crumble bacon when cool; set aside. Reserve 1 tablespoon of bacon drippings.

**Step 2**

Melt butter with drippings in a saucepan over medium heat.

**Step 3**

Cook and stir celery and onion in the saucepan until onion is translucent, about 4 minutes.

**Step 4**

Whisk flour into the mixture and cook for 1 minute.

**Step 5**

Whisk in chicken broth and bring to a boil.

**Step 6**

Add potato and chopped asparagus stalks, reserving the asparagus tips for later. Season with salt and ground black pepper.

**Step 7**

Reduce heat and simmer for 20 minutes.

**Step 8**

Pour the soup into a blender, filling the pitcher no more than halfway full. Hold down the lid of the blender with a folded kitchen towel, and carefully start the blender, using a few quick pulses to get the soup moving before leaving it on to puree. Puree in batches until smooth and pour into a clean pot. Alternately, you can use a stick blender and puree the soup right in the cooking pot.

**Step 9**

Cook and stir mushrooms and asparagus tips in the same skillet used for bacon until mushrooms give up their liquid, 5 to 8 minutes. Season with salt and ground black pepper, if needed.

**Step 10**

Stir mushrooms, asparagus tips, and half-and-half cream to pureed soup. Cook until thoroughly heated.

**Step 11**

Garnish soup with crumbled bacon.

**Nutrition Facts**

**Per Serving:**

155 calories; protein 5.2g 10% DV; carbohydrates 12.7g 4% DV; fat 10g 15% DV; cholesterol 27.4mg 9% DV; sodium 144.9mg 6% DV.

# Strawberry Daiquiri by Request

**Prep:** 5 mins **Total:** 5 mins **Servings:** 2 **Yield:** 2 servings

**Ingredients**

- ½ cup rum
- 2 tablespoons sweetened lime juice (such as Rose's)
- 2 tablespoons grenadine syrup (such as Rose's)
- ½ cup confectioners' sugar
- 2 cups ice cubes
- ½ (16 ounce) package frozen strawberries
- 1 tablespoon whipped cream, divided

**Directions**

**Step 1**

Place the rum, lime juice, grenadine, confectioners' sugar, ice cubes, and strawberries into a blender. Cover, and puree until smooth. Pour into glasses and top each with a dollop of whipped cream, if desired.

**Nutrition Facts**

**Per Serving:**

347.4 calories; protein 0.1g; carbohydrates 50.8g 16% DV; fat 1.4g 2% DV; cholesterol 5.1mg 2% DV; sodium 7.7mg.

# Cremesicle Smoothie

**Prep:** 5 mins **Total:** 5 mins **Servings:** 2 **Yield:** 3 cups

**Ingredients**

- 1 cup orange juice
- 1 cup milk
- 1 cup crushed ice
- 1 teaspoon white sugar, or more to taste

**Directions**

**Step 1**

Blend orange juice, milk, ice, and sugar together in a blender until no large chunks of ice remain.

**Nutrition Facts**

**Per Serving:**

124.9 calories; protein 4.9g 10% DV; carbohydrates 20.7g 7% DV; fat 2.7g 4% DV; cholesterol 9.8mg 3% DV; sodium 51.3mg 2% DV.

# Zucchini Bread, Pumpkin Style

**Prep:** 15 mins **Cook:** 50 mins **Additional:** 10 mins **Total:** 1 hr 15 mins **Servings:** 36 **Yield:** 3 loaves

**Ingredients**

- 3 medium zucchini, cut into chunks
- 4 ¾ cups all-purpose flour
- 1 ½ teaspoons baking powder
- 1 ½ teaspoons baking soda
- 1 ½ teaspoons salt
- 1 ½ teaspoons ground cinnamon
- 1 ½ teaspoons ground nutmeg
- 1 ½ teaspoons ground cloves
- 1 ½ cups vegetable oil
- 6 large eggs eggs
- 4 cups white sugar

**Directions**

**Step 1**

Preheat an oven to 350 degrees F (175 degrees C). Grease and flour 3 9x5 inch loaf pans, and set aside.

**Step 2**

Place the zucchini chunks into a saucepan, and cover with water. Bring to a boil and cook until the zucchini are tender, about 5 minutes. Drain the zucchini, place them in a blender, and blend until they are pureed, about 2 minutes. Let the zucchini puree cool for about 10 minutes.

**Step 3**

Mix the flour, baking powder, baking soda, salt, cinnamon, nutmeg, and cloves in a bowl, and stir to eliminate lumps.

**Step 4**

Place the zucchini puree in a large bowl, and whisk in the oil, eggs, and sugar. Beat in the flour mixture to form a thick batter.

**Step 5**

Divide the batter evenly among the prepared loaf pans, and bake in the preheated oven until the tops are lightly browned and the loaves spring back when gently pressed, 45 minutes to 1 hour. A toothpick inserted into the center should come out clean. Cool in the pans for 10 minutes before removing to cool completely on a wire rack.

**Nutrition Facts**

**Per Serving:**

242.1 calories; protein 3g 6% DV; carbohydrates 35.7g 12% DV; fat 10.2g 16% DV; cholesterol 31mg 10% DV; sodium 183.5mg 7% DV.

# Frozen Banana Margaritas

**Prep:** 15 mins **Total:** 15 mins **Servings:** 8 **Yield:** 8 servings

## Ingredients

- 2 tablespoons lemon juice
- 2 tablespoons lime juice
- ¾ cup banana liqueur
- ½ cup tequila
- ¼ cup triple sec (orange-flavored liqueur)
- 6 ice cubes ice cubes
- 2 large bananas

## Directions

### Step 1

In the container of a blender, combine the lemon juice, lime juice, banana liqueur, tequila, triple sec, and bananas. Add ice cubes until the mixture reaches the 6 cup line. Cover and blend until smooth. Pour into margarita glasses to serve.

## Nutrition Facts

**Per Serving:**

177.6 calories; protein 0.4g 1% DV; carbohydrates 22.5g 8% DV; fat 0.2g; cholesterolmg; sodium 3.1mg.

# Rhubarb Margarita

**Prep:** 10 mins **Cook:** 20 mins **Additional:** 2 hrs **Total:** 2 hrs 30 mins **Servings:** 4 **Yield:** 4 cocktails

## Ingredients

- 4 cups diced rhubarb
- ½ cup water
- ½ cup white sugar
- 4 cups ice
- ⅔ cup tequila

**Directions**

**Step 1**

Place the rhubarb into a saucepan, and pour in the water. Cover, and bring to a simmer over medium heat. Reduce heat to medium-low, and continue simmering until the rhubarb breaks down and releases its juices, about 15 minutes. Strain the juice, and press the pulp to squeeze out as much liquid as you can. Discard the pulp, and stir the sugar into the hot juice. Refrigerate the syrup until very cold, at least 2 hours.

**Step 2**

To prepare the margaritas, place the ice into a blender, then pour in the tequila and rhubarb syrup. Blend until smooth, or until pureed to your desired consistency. Pour into chilled margarita glasses to serve.

**Nutrition Facts**

**Per Serving:**

209.8 calories; protein 1.1g 2% DV; carbohydrates 30.5g 10% DV; fat 0.2g; cholesterolmg; sodium 6.1mg.

# Cilantro Jalapeno Pesto with Lime

**Prep:** 10 mins **Total:** 10 mins **Servings:** 6 **Yield:** 3 /4 cup

**Ingredients**

- 1 bunch fresh cilantro
- 2 ½ tablespoons toasted pine nuts
- ¼ cup extra virgin olive oil
- 5 cloves garlic
- 1 tablespoon fresh lime juice
- ½ fresh jalapeno pepper, seeded
- ¼ cup grated Parmesan cheese

**Directions**

**Step 1**

Combine the cilantro, pine nuts, olive oil, garlic, lime juice, jalapeno pepper, and Parmesan cheese in a blender; pulse until the mixture reaches a soft, paste-like consistency.

# Easy Creamy Caesar Salad Dressing

**Prep:** 15 mins **Total:** 15 mins **Servings:** 8 **Yield:** 8 servings

## Ingredients

- ⅓ cup canola oil
- ⅓ cup grated Parmesan cheese
- ¼ cup egg substitute (such as Egg Beaters)
- 2 teaspoons Dijon mustard
- 1 clove garlic, minced
- ½ teaspoon anchovy paste
- ¼ teaspoon Worcestershire sauce
- ⅛ teaspoon ground black pepper
- 1 pinch salt to taste
- 1 head romaine lettuce, torn into bite-size pieces
- 1 cup croutons

## Directions

### Step 1

Blend vegetable oil, Parmesan cheese, egg substitute, Dijon mustard, garlic, anchovy paste, Worcestershire sauce, and pepper in a blender or food processor until smooth; season with salt.

### Step 2

Drizzle dressing over lettuce in a large mixing bowl; toss to coat. Top salad with croutons.



# World's Best Marinara

**Prep:** 15 mins **Cook:** 40 mins **Total:** 55 mins **Servings:** 8 **Yield:** 8 servings

## Ingredients

- 1 tablespoon olive oil
- 1 sweet onion, diced
- 4 cloves garlic, minced
- 1 (8 ounce) package fresh mushrooms, chopped
- 1 red bell pepper, diced
- 1 cup fresh flat-leaf parsley, torn
- 2 tablespoons oregano
- 2 tablespoons white sugar
- 2 teaspoons dried basil
- 1 teaspoon dried rosemary
- ½ teaspoon dried sage
- ½ teaspoon red pepper flakes
- ½ teaspoon salt
- 1 pinch ground black pepper to taste
- 1 (28 ounce) can tomato sauce

## Directions

### Step 1

Heat olive oil in a saucepan over medium heat; cook and stir onion and garlic until fragrant, about 2 minutes. Add mushrooms, red bell pepper, and parsley; cook and stir until mushrooms are slightly softened, about 2 minutes. Add oregano, sugar, basil, rosemary, sage, red pepper flakes, salt, and black pepper; stir to combine, 2 minutes.

### Step 2

Stir tomato sauce into seasoned onion-mushroom mixture; cook over low heat until flavors have combined, 30 minutes.

### Step 3

Transfer half the sauce to a blender; blend until smooth. Return to saucepan with the remaining sauce; stir to combine.

## Nutrition Facts

### Per Serving:

75.1 calories; protein 2.9g 6% DV; carbohydrates 13g 4% DV; fat 2.2g 3% DV; cholesterolmg; sodium 666.2mg 27% DV.

# Tofu 'Ricotta'

Prep: 5 mins Total: 5 mins Servings: 8 Yield: 8 servings

## Ingredients

- 1 pound extra-firm tofu
- 1 tablespoon garlic powder
- 1 teaspoon oregano
- 1 teaspoon basil
- 1 teaspoon lemon juice
- ¼ cup extra-virgin olive oil, or as needed

## Directions

### Step 1

Blend tofu, garlic powder, oregano, basil, and lemon juice in a blender until combined. Stream olive oil into the tofu mixture while blending until your obtain the desired consistency.

## Nutrition Facts

**Per Serving:**

110.8 calories; protein 4.8g 10% DV; carbohydrates 2.1g 1% DV; fat 9.7g 15% DV; cholesterolmg; sodium 4.3mg.

# Frozen Vanilla Chai Tea

Prep: 10 mins Cook: 5 mins Total: 15 mins Servings: 1 Yield: 1 serving

## Ingredients

- 1 cup water
- 2 eaches chai tea bags
- 2 tablespoons white sugar
- 1 teaspoon ground cinnamon
- 1 teaspoon vanilla extract
- 2 cups ice, divided
- ½ cup milk

## Directions

### Step 1

Bring water and tea to a boil in a saucepan; boil for 3 to 4 minutes. Remove saucepan from heat and stir in sugar, cinnamon, and vanilla extract. Remove tea bags from water.

**Step 2**

Blend 1 cup ice and milk together in a blender until smooth. Add remaining 1 cup ice and chai tea mixture; blend until smooth.

**Cook's Note:**

You may want to cut the tags off the tea bags before boiling. It's okay if a tea bag bursts, that just means you have to strain it later.

**Nutrition Facts**

**Per Serving:**

182.6 calories; protein 4.1g 8% DV; carbohydrates 34.4g 11% DV; fat 2.4g 4% DV; cholesterol 9.8mg 3% DV; sodium 57.8mg 2% DV.

# Mexican Atole

**Prep:** 5 mins **Cook:** 10 mins **Total:** 15 mins **Servings:** 5 **Yield:** 5 cups

**Ingredients**

- ½ cup masa (corn flour)
- 5 cups water
- 1 tablespoon ground cinnamon
- 5 tablespoons piloncillo, brown sugar cones
- 1 tablespoon vanilla extract

**Directions**

**Step 1**

Place the masa, water, cinnamon and piloncillo in a blender. Blend until smooth, about 3 minutes.

**Step 2**

Pour the contents of the blender into a sauce pan and bring the mixture to boil over medium heat, stirring constantly. When the mixture reaches a boil, turn the heat to low and continue to whisk for 5 minutes.

**Step 3**

Remove the pan from the heat and stir in the vanilla. Pour into mugs and serve hot.

**Nutrition Facts**

**Per Serving:**

67.5 calories; protein 1.1g 2% DV; carbohydrates 14.1g 5% DV; fat 0.4g 1% DV; cholesterolmg; sodium 8mg.

# Cocojito (Frozen Mojito)

**Prep:** 10 mins **Total:** 10 mins **Servings:** 2 **Yield:** 2 servings

**Ingredients**

- 4 cups ice cubes
- 2 ½ fruit (2" dia)s limes, rind removed
- 7 fluid ounces sweetened cream of coconut (such as Coco Lopez)
- 2 ½ (1.5 fluid ounce) jiggers white rum (such as Bacardi)
- 5 sprigs fresh mint leaves
- 2 sprig (blank)s mint sprigs, for garnish
- 2 wedge (blank)s lime wedges, for garnish

**Directions**

**Step 1**

Blend the ice, limes, cream of coconut, rum, and mint leaves together in a blender until smooth. Pour into two glasses and garnish each with a mint sprig and lime wedge as desired.

**Nutrition Facts**

**Per Serving:**

585.5 calories; protein 2.4g 5% DV; carbohydrates 74.8g 24% DV; fat 20.1g 31% DV; cholesterolmg; sodium 59.4mg 2% DV.

# Sweet Potato and Banana Smoothie

**Prep:** 10 mins **Cook:** 1 hr **Additional:** 8 hrs **Total:** 9 hrs 10 mins **Servings:** 2 **Yield:** 2 servings

**Ingredients**

- 1 large sweet potato
- 1 banana
- 2 cups soy milk
- ¼ teaspoon ground cinnamon

**Directions**

**Step 1**

Preheat oven to 350 degrees F (175 degrees C).

**Step 2**

Bake sweet potato in the preheated oven until tender and cooked through, about 1 hour.

Remove peel from cooked sweet potato and cool in the refrigerator 8 hours or overnight.

**Step 3**

Blend sweet potato, banana, soy milk, and cinnamon together in a blender until smooth.

Cook's Note:

You can also microwave the sweet potato for about 10 minutes instead of baking it.

Peel the cooked sweet potato before or after cooling it.

**Nutrition Facts**

**Per Serving:**

379.7 calories; protein 12.2g 24% DV; carbohydrates 74.6g 24% DV; fat 4.6g 7% DV; cholesterolmg; sodium 249.4mg 10% DV.

# Garden-Fresh Tomato Soup

**Prep:** 20 mins **Cook:** 55 mins **Total:** 1 hr 15 mins **Servings:** 4 **Yield:** 4 servings

**Ingredients**

- 7 cups chopped fresh tomatoes (with seeds and juice)
- 1 onion, finely chopped
- 1 cup finely chopped carrots

- 3 cloves garlic, crushed
- 1 teaspoon extra-virgin olive oil, or more to taste
- 2 cups chicken broth
- 2 teaspoons salt, or to taste
- ¾ teaspoon white sugar
- ¾ teaspoon dried dill weed
- ½ teaspoon ground black pepper
- ¼ teaspoon celery salt
- ¼ teaspoon ground cloves
- 1 cup skim milk
- 1 tablespoon cornstarch
- 1 ½ teaspoons butter
- 5 large fresh basil leaves, or more to taste
- ¼ cup grated Parmesan cheese, or to taste
- 2 tablespoons shredded fresh basil, or to taste

**Directions**

**Step 1**

Combine tomatoes, onion, carrots, and garlic in a large pot. Drizzle olive oil over tomato mixture; cook and stir over medium heat. Cover pot and simmer, stirring occasionally, until vegetables are tender, about 25 minutes.

**Step 2**

Mix chicken broth, salt, sugar, dill, black pepper, celery salt, and cloves into tomato mixture. Cover pot and simmer, stirring occasionally, until soup flavors have blended, about 20 minutes.

**Step 3**

Whisk milk and cornstarch together in a bowl until dissolved.

**Step 4**

Heat butter in a saucepan over medium-low heat. Whisk cornstarch mixture into melted butter until smooth and thickened, 3 to 5 minutes.

**Step 5**

Slowly pour cornstarch mixture into tomato soup, stirring until incorporated.

**Step 6**

Pour half of the soup and basil leaves into a blender no more than half-full. Cover and hold lid down; pulse a few times before leaving on to blend. Puree soup in batches until smooth. Return blended soup to pot and heat on low for 3 to 5 minutes. Spoon soup into serving bowls and top with Parmesan cheese and shredded basil.

**Cook's Note:**

You may add a splash of balsamic vinegar in individual bowls when serving, if desired.

**Nutrition Facts**

**Per Serving:**

160.4 calories; protein 7.7g 15% DV; carbohydrates 24.2g 8% DV; fat 5g 8% DV; cholesterol 9.7mg 3% DV; sodium 1408.8mg 56% DV.

# Watermelon Refreshing Green Smoothie

**Prep:** 10 mins **Total:** 10 mins **Servings:** 1 **Yield:** 1 smoothie

**Ingredients**

- 2 cups diced watermelon
- ½ cup fresh spinach
- ¼ cup broccoli florets
- ¼ cucumber, sliced
- ½ apple - peeled, cored, and diced, or more to taste
- 1 stalk celery, coarsely chopped

**Directions**

**Step 1**

Place watermelon in a blender; mix until liquefied. Add spinach, broccoli, cucumber, apple, and celery; blend until smooth.

**Cook's Note:**

Watermelon is used instead of water, so the more you use the lighter and sweeter it will be.

**Nutrition Facts**

**Per Serving:**

64.1 calories; protein 2g 4% DV; carbohydrates 15.3g 5% DV; fat 0.4g 1% DV; cholesterolmg; sodium 53.5mg 2% DV.

# Mashed Cauliflower (Mashed Potatoes Replacement)

Prep: 15 mins Cook: 15 mins Total: 30 mins Servings: 6 Yield: 6 servings

Ingredients

- 2 pounds cauliflower, cut into 1-inch pieces
- ¼ cup heavy cream
- ⅓ cup freshly grated Parmesan cheese
- ¼ cup unsalted butter
- ¼ cup reduced-fat cream cheese
- 1 teaspoon sea salt

**Directions**

**Step 1**

Bring a pot of water to a boil. Add cauliflower and reduce heat to medium. Cook cauliflower until very tender, about 10 minutes; drain, shaking the colander to remove as much water as possible.

**Step 2**

Blend drained cauliflower and cream in a blender until smooth; transfer to a pot over low heat.

**Step 3**

Stir Parmesan cheese, butter, cream cheese, and sea salt through the blended cauliflower; cook and stir until hot, about 5 minutes.

**Nutrition Facts**

**Per Serving:**

183.6 calories; protein 6.1g 12% DV; carbohydrates 9.2g 3% DV; fat 14.6g 23% DV; cholesterol 43.8mg 15% DV; sodium 496.4mg 20% DV.

# Coconut Curry Pumpkin Soup

**Prep:** 20 mins **Additional:** 30 mins **Total:** 50 mins **Servings:** 6 **Yield:** 6 servings

**Ingredients**

- ¼ cup coconut oil
- 1 cup chopped onions
- 1 clove garlic, minced
- 3 cups vegetable broth
- 1 teaspoon curry powder
- ½ teaspoon salt
- ¼ teaspoon ground coriander
- ¼ teaspoon crushed red pepper flakes
- 1 (15 ounce) can 100% pure pumpkin
- 1 cup light coconut milk

**Directions**

**Step 1**

Heat the coconut oil in a deep pot over medium-high heat. Stir in the onions and garlic; cook until the onions are translucent, about 5 minutes. Mix in the vegetable broth, curry powder, salt, coriander, and red pepper flakes. Cook and stir until the mixture comes to a gentle boil, about 10 minutes. Cover, and boil 15 to 20 minutes more, stirring occasionally. Whisk in the pumpkin and coconut milk, and cook another 5 minutes.

**Step 2**

Pour the soup into a blender, filling only half way and working in batches if necessary; process until smooth. Return to a pot, and reheat briefly over medium heat before serving.

**Nutrition Facts**

**Per Serving:**

170.7 calories; protein 2g 4% DV; carbohydrates 12g 4% DV; fat 13.5g 21% DV; cholesterolmg; sodium 600.6mg 24% DV.

# Horchata

**Prep:** 15 mins **Additional:** 3 hrs **Total:** 3 hrs 15 mins **Servings:** 8 **Yield:** 2 quarts

**Ingredients**

- 2 quarts hot water
- ½ cup white sugar
- 1 ½ teaspoons ground cinnamon
- 1 cup long grain rice

- 1 cup milk
- 1 quart ice cubes, for serving

**Directions**

**Step 1**

Pour sugar, cinnamon, and rice into hot water; stir until sugar dissolves. Cover, and let stand at room temperature for at least 3 hours, but preferably overnight.

**Step 2**

Stir in milk, then puree with a hand blender, or in batches in a standing blender until the rice resembles fine sand. Strain through several layers of cheesecloth, or through a very fine strainer. Serve over ice.

**Nutrition Facts**

**Per Serving:**

149.1 calories; protein 2.7g 5% DV; carbohydrates 32.8g 11% DV; fat 0.8g 1% DV; cholesterol 2.4mg 1% DV; sodium 24.5mg 1% DV.

# Dane's Frozen Peach Margaritas

**Prep:** 10 mins **Total:** 10 mins **Servings:** 3 **Yield:** 3 servings

**Ingredients**

- 2 cups ice cubes, or as desired
- 1 fresh peach, pitted and sliced
- 2 ½ (1.5 fluid ounce) jiggers tequila
- 1 (1.5 fluid ounce) jigger triple sec
- 1 (1.5 fluid ounce) jigger peach schnapps
- 1 lime, juiced
- 1 tablespoon agave nectar

**Directions**

**Step 1**

Blend ice cubes, peach, tequila, triple sec, peach schnapps, lime juice, and agave nectar together in a blender until smooth, about 30 seconds.

**Nutrition Facts**

**Per Serving:**

218.3 calories; protein 0.1g; carbohydrates 21.7g 7% DV; fat 0.1g; cholesterolmg; sodium 8.8mg.

# Banana Ice Cream from Almond Breeze

**Prep:** 15 mins **Total:** 15 mins **Servings:** 4 **Yield:** 4 servings

**Ingredients**

- ¼ cup Almond Breeze Almondmilk Vanilla
- 3 eaches bananas, cut into 1-inch chunks & frozen
- 2 tablespoons peanut butter
- 2 tablespoons chocolate chips

**Directions**

**Step 1**

In a food processor or blender, mix frozen banana chunks, Almond Breeze Almondmilk Vanilla, peanut butter, and chocolate chips.

**Step 2**

Blend until smooth.

**Nutrition Facts**

**Per Serving:**

200.7 calories; protein 3.7g 7% DV; carbohydrates 31.8g 10% DV; fat 8.8g 14% DV; cholesterolmg; sodium 51mg 2% DV.

# Nutella Coffee Shake

**Prep:** 10 mins **Total:** 10 mins **Servings:** 2 **Yield:** 2 servings

**Ingredients**

- 2 cups ice cubes
- 1 ½ cups milk
- 3 tablespoons white sugar
- 2 tablespoons chocolate-hazelnut spread (such as Nutella)
- 4 teaspoons instant coffee granules

- 1 tablespoon vanilla extract

**Directions**

**Step 1**

Blend ice, milk, sugar, chocolate-hazelnut spread, instant coffee, and vanilla extract together in a blender until desired consistency is reached, about 30 seconds.

**Nutrition Facts**

**Per Serving:**

266.8 calories; protein 7.3g 15% DV; carbohydrates 38.3g 12% DV; fat 8.1g 13% DV; cholesterol 14.6mg 5% DV; sodium 91.2mg 4% DV.

# Vitamix Green Smoothie

**Prep:** 10 mins **Total:** 10 mins **Servings:** 4 **Yield:** 4 servings

**Ingredients**

- 1 ½ cups water
- 15 grape, seedlesses seedless red grapes, or more to taste
- 1 frozen banana
- ½ pear, peeled
- 1 orange, peeled and seeded
- ¼ cup fresh spinach
- 1 teaspoon ground flax seeds
- 3 cubes ice cubes

**Directions**

**Step 1**

Pour water into your Vitamix blender. Add grapes, banana, pear, orange, spinach, ground flax seeds, and ice, in that order. Blend until smooth and creamy.

**Cook's Note:**

If you are using a regular blender, you may need to add ingredients one at a time to make sure it blends well.

**Nutrition Facts**

**Per Serving:**

75.1 calories; protein 1.1g 2% DV; carbohydrates 18.5g 6% DV; fat 0.6g 1% DV; cholesterolmg; sodium 5.7mg.

# 'Secret' Salad Dressing

**Prep:** 10 mins **Total:** 10 mins **Servings:** 16 **Yield:** 2 cups

**Ingredients**

- ½ cup ketchup
- 1 cup vegetable oil
- ¼ cup mayonnaise
- ¼ cup white vinegar
- ¼ cup white sugar
- ¼ cup diced onion
- 1 teaspoon salt
- ¼ teaspoon pepper

**Directions**

**Step 1**

Combine the ketchup, vegetable oil, mayonnaise, vinegar, sugar, onion, salt, and pepper in a blender; blend until smooth. Store in refrigerator.

**Nutrition Facts**

**Per Serving:**

166.8 calories; protein 0.2g; carbohydrates 5.4g 2% DV; fat 16.5g 25% DV; cholesterol 1.3mg; sodium 248.5mg 10% DV.

# Sushi House Salad Dressing, It's ORANGE!

**Prep:** 10 mins **Total:** 10 mins **Servings:** 8 **Yield:** cup

**Ingredients**

- 3 carrot, (7-1/2")s carrots, peeled and cut in chunks
- 1 (2 inch) piece fresh ginger root
- 1 tablespoon soy sauce
- ¼ cup white wine vinegar
- ¼ cup orange juice
- 2 tablespoons peanut oil

**Directions**

**Step 1**

Place carrots, ginger root, soy sauce, vinegar, and orange juice into a blender; blend until liquified. Pour in peanut oil and pulse once or twice just to combine.

**Nutrition Facts**

**Per Serving:**

46.7 calories; protein 0.5g 1% DV; carbohydrates 3.8g 1% DV; fat 3.5g 5% DV; cholesterolmg; sodium 132.4mg 5% DV.

# Heavenly Honeydew Juice

**Prep:** 10 mins **Total:** 10 mins **Servings:** 6 **Yield:** 6 servings

**Ingredients**

- 1 (5 pound) honeydew melon, quartered and seeded
- 2 cups ice cubes
- 1 cup water
- 3 tablespoons white sugar

**Directions**

**Step 1**

Scrape flesh from honeydew melon quarters into a blender; add ice cubes, water, and sugar. Blend until smooth and sugar has dissolved. Serve immediately.

**Nutrition Facts**

**Per Serving:**

159.2 calories; protein 2g 4% DV; carbohydrates 40.3g 13% DV; fat 0.5g 1% DV; cholesterolmg; sodium 68.7mg 3% DV.

# Vegetarian Potato-Leek Soup

**Prep:** 20 mins **Cook:** 35 mins **Total:** 55 mins **Servings:** 8 **Yield:** 8 servings

**Ingredients**

- ¼ cup olive oil, divided
- 2 leeks leeks, chopped
- 1 (32 fluid ounce) container vegetable broth
- 1 ¾ cups water
- 2 pounds potatoes, cut into cubes
- ⅜ teaspoon cayenne pepper
- ¼ teaspoon salt

**Directions**

**Step 1**

Heat 2 tablespoons olive oil in a stock pot over medium heat. Cook and stir leeks in hot oil until completely softened, adding remaining olive oil in small amounts as you cook the leeks, about 10 minutes.

**Step 2**

Pour vegetable broth and water into the pot; add potatoes. Bring mixture to a boil, reduce heat to medium-low, and cook at a simmer until the potatoes are completely tender, about 25 minutes.

**Step 3**

Pour potato mixture into a blender no more than half full. Cover and hold lid down; pulse a few times before leaving on to blend. Puree in batches until smooth. Stir cayenne pepper and salt into the soup.

**Nutrition Facts**

**Per Serving:**

175.9 calories; protein 3.1g 6% DV; carbohydrates 25.5g 8% DV; fat 7.2g 11% DV; cholesterolmg; sodium 315.6mg 13% DV.

# Rob Roy

**Prep:** 5 mins **Total:** 5 mins **Servings:** 1 **Yield:** 1 drink

**Ingredients**

- ¼ cup blended Scotch whiskey
- 2 tablespoons sweet vermouth
- 4 ice cubes ice cubes
- 2 dashes Angostura bitters
- 1 maraschino cherry

**Directions**

**Step 1**

Pour Scotch and vermouth into a glass with ice cubes. Shake in bitters, stir, and garnish with a maraschino cherry.

**Nutrition Facts**

**Per Serving:**

207.2 calories; protein 0.1g; carbohydrates 7.7g 3% DV; fatg; cholesterolmg; sodium 5.4mg.

# Mango Peach Banana Smoothie

**Prep:** 10 mins **Total:** 10 mins **Servings:** 4 **Yield:** 4 servings

**Ingredients**

- 1 (16 ounce) can mango nectar
- 1 cup peach yogurt
- 1 cup vanilla frozen yogurt
- 1 ½ cups frozen peach slices
- 1 frozen banana, cut into chunks

**Directions**

**Step 1**

Combine mango nectar, peach yogurt, and frozen yogurt in pitcher of a blender; add peach slices and banana chunks. Blend until smooth, 30 seconds to 1 minute.

**Nutrition Facts**

**Per Serving:**

322.1 calories; protein 6.9g 14% DV; carbohydrates 74.8g 24% DV; fat 1g 2% DV; cholesterol 5.5mg 2% DV; sodium 71.9mg 3% DV.

# Chayote Soup

**Prep:** 30 mins **Cook:** 30 mins **Total:** 1 hr **Servings:** 4 **Yield:** 4 servings

## Ingredients

- 2 cubes chicken bouillon, crumbled
- 2 cups hot water
- 1 tablespoon unsalted butter
- 1 small yellow onion, minced
- 3 cloves garlic, minced
- ¼ teaspoon crushed red pepper flakes
- 2 chayote, (5-3/4")s chayote squashes, peeled and cut into 1/2-inch pieces
- 2 tablespoons chopped fresh cilantro
- 1 pinch salt and ground black pepper to taste
- 1 tablespoon chopped fresh cilantro

## Directions

### Step 1

Dissolve the bouillon in the hot water.

### Step 2

Melt the butter in a large saucepan over medium heat. Cook and stir the onion, garlic, and red pepper in the butter until the onion is soft. Add the squash, 2 tablespoons cilantro, salt, and pepper and stir continually for 5 minutes. Stir in the bouillon mixture and 1 tablespoon cilantro; cover. Simmer about 20 minutes.

### Step 3

Pour the mixture into a blender and puree until smooth. Pour into bowls and garnish with a sprig of cilantro to serve.

### Nutrition Facts

**Per Serving:**

60.9 calories; protein 1.6g 3% DV; carbohydrates 7.7g 3% DV; fat 3.2g 5% DV; cholesterol 7.9mg 3% DV; sodium 604.2mg 24% DV.

# Watermelon Pink Lemonade

**Prep:** 5 mins **Total:** 5 mins **Servings:** 1 **Yield:** 1 cup

## Ingredients

- 1 cup water
- 2 tablespoons lemon juice
- 4 teaspoons white sugar
- 1 small slice (0.5 oz) watermelon

**Directions**

**Step 1**

Combine water, lemon juice, sugar, and watermelon in a blender. Blend until smooth.

**Cook's Note:**

You may substitute honey for the sugar.

**Nutrition Facts**

**Per Serving:**

76.2 calories; protein 0.2g; carbohydrates 20.3g 7% DV; fatg; cholesterolmg; sodium 7.6mg.

# Strawberry Basil Margarita

**Prep:** 5 mins **Total:** 5 mins **Servings:** 2 **Yield:** 2 cocktails

**Ingredients**

- 1 cup hulled strawberries
- ¼ cup tequila
- 1 tablespoon orange-flavored liqueur, such as Cointreau
- 1 tablespoon lemon juice
- 2 tablespoons white sugar
- 3 large basil leaves
- 8 eaches ice cubes

**Directions**

**Step 1**

Combine the strawberries, tequila, orange-flavored liqueur, lemon juice, sugar, and basil leaves in a blender; mix on low until smooth. Add the ice and puree until the ice is crushed, 30 to 60 seconds.

**Nutrition Facts**

**Per Serving:**

163.9 calories; protein 0.5g 1% DV; carbohydrates 21.8g 7% DV; fat 0.2g; cholesterolmg; sodium 4.1mg.

# Watermelon Frose

**Prep:** 15 mins **Cook:** 7 mins **Additional:** 8 hrs 15 mins **Total:** 8 hrs 37 mins **Servings:** 4

**Yield:** 4 drinks

**Ingredients**

- 1 (750 milliliter) bottle rose wine
- 1 pound cubed seeded watermelon
- ½ cup water
- ½ cup white sugar
- 6 leaves fresh basil
- ¼ cup freshly squeezed lime juice

**Directions**

**Step 1**

Pour rose wine into ice cube trays. Freeze until solid, 8 hours to overnight.

**Step 2**

Line a baking sheet with parchment paper. Spread out watermelon cubes so they are not touching. Freeze until firm, at least 2 hours. Transfer to a resealable plastic bag. Return to the freezer.

**Step 3**

Combine water and sugar in a small saucepan over medium heat. Stir constantly until sugar dissolves, 2 to 3 minutes. Add basil; bring to a boil. Remove from heat and let steep for 15 minutes. Strain simple syrup into a jar with a lid. Discard basil leaves. Place in the refrigerator.

**Step 4**

Place rose ice cubes, frozen watermelon, chilled simple syrup, and lime juice in a large blender; blend until combined and smooth. Pour into glasses.

**Cook's Note:**

This recipe works best with darker rose wines, such as Pinot Noir or Merlot varieties.

**Nutrition Facts**

# Nona's Japanese Ume Dressing

**Prep:** 15 mins **Total:** 15 mins **Servings:** 8 **Yield:** 1 cup

## Ingredients

- ½ cup vegetable oil
- ¼ cup chopped onion
- ¼ cup rice vinegar
- 1 tablespoon toasted sesame seeds
- 1 tablespoon minced fresh ginger root
- 1 tablespoon umeboshi, minced
- 1 ½ teaspoons lemon juice
- 1 teaspoon white sugar, or more to taste
- 1 teaspoon salt
- 1 pinch ground black pepper to taste

## Directions

### Step 1

Place the vegetable oil, onion, rice vinegar, sesame seeds, ginger, umeboshi, lemon juice, sugar, salt, and pepper into a blender. Cover, and puree until smooth, about 30 seconds.

## Nutrition Facts



# Nobody's Strawberry Watermelon Shakedown

**Prep:** 5 mins **Total:** 5 mins **Servings:** 1 **Yield:** 1 large glass

## Ingredients

- 1 ½ cups frozen strawberries
- 1 ½ cups frozen diced watermelon
- ¼ cup cream
- ¼ cup plain yogurt
- 2 tablespoons orange juice
- 1 tablespoon white sugar

- ¼ teaspoon vanilla extract

**Directions**

**Step 1**

Blend the strawberries, watermelon, cream, yogurt, orange juice, sugar, and vanilla in a blender until smooth.

**Nutrition Facts**

**Per Serving:**

493.7 calories; protein 7.5g 15% DV; carbohydrates 69.3g 22% DV; fat 23.7g 37% DV; cholesterol 85.2mg 28% DV; sodium 74.8mg 3% DV.

# Celery Root Puree

**Prep:** 15 mins **Cook:** 15 mins **Total:** 30 mins **Servings:** 6 **Yield:** 6 servings

**Ingredients**

- 1 large celery root, peeled and cut into chunks
- 1 lemon, juiced, divided
- 1 pinch kosher salt to taste
- ⅓ cup heavy whipping cream
- 2 tablespoons butter
- 1 pinch cayenne pepper, or to taste

**Directions**

**Step 1**

Place celery root, 1/2 of the lemon juice, and kosher salt in a large pot and cover with water; bring to a boil. Reduce heat to medium-low and simmer until tender, 15 to 20 minutes. Drain.

**Step 2**

Blend celery root, cream, and butter in a blender until smooth. Push puree into a bowl through a fine-mesh strainer with a wooden spoon or spatula until puree is completely smooth. Drizzle remaining lemon juice into puree and season with salt and cayenne pepper.

**Cook's Note:**

You can substitute milk for the heavy whipping cream, if desired.

**Nutrition Facts**

**Per Serving:**

139.4 calories; protein 2.5g 5% DV; carbohydrates 14.7g 5% DV; fat 9.2g 14% DV; cholesterol 28.3mg 9% DV; sodium 232.9mg 9% DV.

# Tropical Sunshine Smoothie

**Prep:** 10 mins **Total:** 10 mins **Servings:** 2 **Yield:** 2 servings

## Ingredients

- 1 banana
- ½ cup orange juice
- ½ cup cubed fresh mango
- ½ cup cubed fresh pineapple
- ½ cup coconut water
- ½ teaspoon freshly squeezed lime juice
- 1 sprig fresh chocolate mint, finely chopped

## Directions

**Step 1**

Blend banana, orange juice, mango, pineapple, coconut water, lime juice, mint in a blender until smooth.

**Nutrition Facts**

**Per Serving:**

140 calories; protein 2g 4% DV; carbohydrates 34.8g 11% DV; fat 0.6g 1% DV; cholesterolmg; sodium 65.5mg 3% DV.

# Coconut Avocado Smoothie

**Prep:** 5 mins **Total:** 5 mins **Servings:** 2 **Yield:** 2 servings

## Ingredients

- 1 Hass avocado, diced
- ½ cup low-fat vanilla yogurt
- ½ cup whole milk
- ¼ cup cream of coconut
- 8 eaches ice cubes

**Directions**

**Step 1**

Combine avocado, yogurt, milk, cream of coconut, and ice cubes in a blender; blend until smooth.

**Cook's Notes**

Please make sure that you use cream of coconut. It is thick like sweetened condensed milk. Using coconut milk or coconut water will dramatically affect the outcome and should not be used. Cream of coconut can be found in your grocery store with the cocktail mixes or with the foreign foods.

Add more milk if you like your smoothie thinner, more ice if you like it thicker.

**Nutrition Facts**

**Per Serving:**

356.6 calories; protein 7.3g 15% DV; carbohydrates 35.7g 12% DV; fat 22.4g 34% DV; cholesterol 9.2mg 3% DV; sodium 85.2mg 3% DV.

# Healthy Strawberry Smoothie

**Prep:** 10 mins **Total:** 10 mins **Servings:** 2 **Yield:** 2 servings

**Ingredients**

- 1 cup almond milk
- 1 banana
- ½ cup frozen strawberries
- ⅓ cup plain fat-free Greek yogurt
- 3 tablespoons rolled oats
- 1 tablespoon slivered almonds

**Directions**

**Step 1**

Blend almond milk, banana, strawberries, yogurt, oats, and almonds together in a NutriBullet or blender until smooth.

**Nutrition Facts**

**Per Serving:**

173.5 calories; protein 6.4g 13% DV; carbohydrates 30.1g 10% DV; fat 3.8g 6% DV; cholesterolmg; sodium 96.3mg 4% DV.

# Pumpkin Pie Smoothie for 2

**Prep:** 5 mins **Total:** 5 mins **Servings:** 2 **Yield:** 2 servings

## Ingredients

- 8 ice cubes ice cubes, or as desired
- 1 banana
- ¼ cup yogurt
- ¼ cup pumpkin puree
- ⅛ teaspoon ground cinnamon
- 1 pinch ground ginger

## Directions

**Step 1**

Blend ice cubes, banana, yogurt, pumpkin, cinnamon, and ginger together in a blender until smooth.

**Cook's Note:**

Add a splash of milk if the texture is too thick for you liking.

**Nutrition Facts**

**Per Serving:**

84.3 calories; protein 2.6g 5% DV; carbohydrates 18.6g 6% DV; fat 0.8g 1% DV; cholesterol 1.8mg 1% DV; sodium 98.5mg 4% DV.

# Garlic and Basil Vinaigrette

**Prep:** 10 mins **Total:** 10 mins **Servings:** 8 **Yield:** 1 cup

## Ingredients

- ½ cup fresh basil leaves, chopped
- 2 tablespoons chopped fresh garlic
- ¼ cup balsamic vinegar
- 3 tablespoons grated Parmesan cheese
- ⅔ cup olive oil

- ½ teaspoon salt
- ½ teaspoon black pepper

**Directions**

**Step 1**

Combine the basil, garlic, balsamic vinegar, and Parmesan cheese in a blender. Blend until ingredients form a paste. Slowly pour olive oil into the mixture and continue to blend until smooth.

**Step 2**

Add salt and pepper to taste. Whisk before serving.

**Nutrition Facts**

**Per Serving:**

176.1 calories; protein 1g 2% DV; carbohydrates 2.1g 1% DV; fat 18.6g 29% DV; cholesterol 1.7mg 1% DV; sodium 176.8mg 7% DV.

# Spicy Avocado Sauce

**Prep:** 10 mins **Total:** 10 mins **Servings:** 6 **Yield:** 1 1/2 cups

**Ingredients**

- 5 medium (blank)s fresh tomatillos, husks removed
- 4 peppers serrano chile peppers, or to taste
- 2 tablespoons chopped fresh cilantro
- 1 ripe avocado - peeled, pitted, and quartered
- 1 pinch salt to taste

**Directions**

**Step 1**

Blend the tomatillos, serrano chile peppers, and cilantro in a blender until smooth. Add 1 avocado quarter and continue blending until the avocado is fully incorporated into the mixture; repeat with each piece of avocado. Season with salt; continue processing until smooth. Serve immediately.

**Nutrition Facts**

**Per Serving:**

64.2 calories; protein 1g 2% DV; carbohydrates 4.8g 2% DV; fat 5.2g 8% DV; cholesterolmg; sodium 3.5mg.

# Banana Monkey

**Prep:** 5 mins **Total:** 5 mins **Servings:** 1 **Yield:** 1 drink

**Ingredients**

- 1 cup pina colada mix
- 1 fluid ounce coffee-flavored liqueur (such as Kahlua)
- 1 fluid ounce vodka
- ⅓ banana, mashed
- 1 cup ice cubes

**Directions**

**Step 1**

Place pina colada mix, coffee-flavored liqueur, vodka, banana, and 1/2 cup of ice into a blender. Cover, and puree until smooth. Add ice a little at a time and repeat until drink reaches desired consistency.

**Nutrition Facts**

**Per Serving:**

460 calories; protein 1.5g 3% DV; carbohydrates 74.6g 24% DV; fat 4.8g 7% DV; cholesterolmg; sodium 27.1mg 1% DV.

# Green Tomato and Pepper Relish

**Prep:** 30 mins **Cook:** 25 mins **Additional:** 2 hrs 20 mins **Total:** 3 hrs 15 mins **Servings:** 64

**Yield:** 6 pints

**Ingredients**

- 12 large green tomatoes, cut into large chunks
- 6 large green bell peppers, cut into large chunks
- 6 large red bell peppers, cut into large chunks
- 10 large onions, cut into large chunks
- 4 cups boiling water, or as needed
- 4 cups vinegar
- 5 cups white sugar
- 1 tablespoon salt
- 2 teaspoons ground turmeric
- 1 (8 ounce) jar mustard
- 6 eaches (1 pint) canning jars with lids and rings

**Directions**

**Step 1**

Place green tomatoes, green bell peppers, red bell peppers, and onions in a food processor; pulse until coarsely chopped. Transfer to a large bowl. Pour boiling water over vegetable mixture; drain. Transfer vegetable mixture to a large pot. Add vinegar, sugar, salt, turmeric, and mustard; stir to combine. Bring mixture to a boil until vegetables are softened, 10 minutes.

**Step 2**

Sterilize the jars, lids, and rings in boiling water for at least 5 minutes. Pack the relish into the hot, sterilized jars, filling the jars to within 1/4 inch of the top. Run a knife or a thin spatula around the insides of the jars after they have been filled to remove any air bubbles. Wipe the rims of the jars with a moist paper towel to remove any food residue. Top with lids, and screw on rings.

**Step 3**

Place a rack in the bottom of a large stockpot and fill halfway with water. Bring to a boil and lower jars into the boiling water using a holder. Leave a 2-inch space between the jars. Pour in more boiling water if necessary to bring the water level to at least 1 inch above the tops of the jars. Bring the water to a rolling boil, cover the pot, and process for 15 minutes.

**Step 4**

Remove the jars from the stockpot and place onto a cloth-covered or wood surface, several inches apart, until cool. Once cool, press the top of each lid with a finger, ensuring that the seal is tight (lid does not move up or down at all). Store in a cool, dark area.

**Nutrition Facts**

**Per Serving:**

88.4 calories; protein 1.1g 2% DV; carbohydrates 21.4g 7% DV; fat 0.3g 1% DV; cholesterolmg; sodium 155.7mg 6% DV.

# Hawaiian Punch Slush for Adults

**Prep:** 15 mins **Total:** 15 mins **Servings:** 8 **Yield:** 2 quarts

**Ingredients**

- 2 (14 ounce) cans cream of coconut
- 3 (6 ounce) cans frozen lemonade concentrate
- 1 (46 fluid ounce) can unsweetened pineapple juice
- 1 (750 milliliter) bottle vodka
- 2 liters lemon-lime flavored carbonated beverage

**Directions**

**Step 1**

In a plastic container combine cream of coconut, lemonade concentrate, pineapple juice and vodka. Mix well and store overnight in the freezer.

**Step 2**

To serve, place 2 scoops in a glass, then fill the glass with lemon-lime soda.

**Nutrition Facts**

**Per Serving:**

886.9 calories; protein 2g 4% DV; carbohydrates 137.3g 46% DV; fat 16.4g 25% DV; cholesterolmg; sodium 69mg 3% DV.

# Habanero Sauce

**Prep:** 15 mins **Total:** 15 mins **Servings:** 25 **Yield:** 3 cups

## Ingredients

- 6 peppers habanero peppers, seeded and chopped, or to taste
- 4 cloves garlic, minced
- 1 (15 ounce) can sliced peaches, drained
- ¼ cup dark molasses
- ¼ cup honey
- ¼ cup brown sugar
- 1 cup distilled white vinegar
- 2 tablespoons spicy brown mustard (such as Gulden's)
- 2 tablespoons paprika
- 1 tablespoon kosher salt
- 1 tablespoon black pepper
- 1 tablespoon ground cumin
- ½ teaspoon ground coriander
- ½ teaspoon ground ginger
- ½ teaspoon ground allspice
- 1 teaspoon liquid smoke flavoring

## Directions

**Step 1**

Place the habanero peppers and garlic into a blender. Puree until the peppers are finely chopped. Add the peaches, molasses, honey, brown sugar, vinegar, mustard, paprika, salt, black pepper, cumin, coriander, ginger, allspice, and liquid smoke. Continue to puree until smooth.

**Nutrition Facts**

**Per Serving:**

43.2 calories; protein 0.4g 1% DV; carbohydrates 10.3g 3% DV; fat 0.4g 1% DV; cholesterolmg; sodium 249.6mg 10% DV.

# Dad's Brandy Ice

**Prep:** 10 mins **Total:** 10 mins **Servings:** 12 **Yield:** 1 half-gallon

## Ingredients

- 6 fluid ounces brandy
- 1 fluid ounce triple sec
- 1 fluid ounce creme de cacao
- 1 fluid ounce honey- and herb-flavored whiskey liqueur (such as Drambuie)
- ½ gallon vanilla ice cream, softened, divided

## Directions

### Step 1

Mix brandy, triple sec, creme de cacao, and whiskey liqueur in a glass measuring cup.

### Step 2

Put about half the vanilla ice cream and half the brandy mixture in a blender; blend until smooth. Add remaining ice cream and brandy mixture; blend again until smooth. Store in freezer in the ice cream container.

## Nutrition Facts

**Per Serving:**

245.5 calories; protein 3.1g 6% DV; carbohydrates 24.2g 8% DV; fat 9.7g 15% DV; cholesterol 38.7mg 13% DV; sodium 71mg 3% DV.

# Sambal Sauce

**Prep:** 25 mins **Cook:** 20 mins **Total:** 45 mins **Servings:** 16 **Yield:** 2 cups

## Ingredients

- 1 cup chopped serrano chiles, with seeds
- 2 tablespoons white sugar
- 2 tablespoons salt
- 1 tablespoon belacan shrimp paste
- 1 tomato, chopped
- ½ onion, chopped
- 1 bulb garlic, peeled and crushed
- 2 tablespoons fresh lime juice
- 2 tablespoons vegetable oil
- 2 stalk (blank)s lemongrass, bruised
- 2 leaf (blank)s fresh curry leaves
- 1 (1/2 inch) piece galangal, thinly sliced
- 2 tablespoons tamarind juice

**Directions**

**Step 1**

Place serrano peppers, sugar, salt, shrimp paste, tomato, onion, garlic, and lime juice into a blender, and blend until smooth. Heat vegetable oil in a saucepan over medium-high heat. Stir in the chile puree along with the lemongrass, curry leaves, and galangal. Cook and stir until the mixture changes color and becomes very fragrant, about 15 minutes. Stir in the tamarind juice, and cook for 1 minute more. Strain before serving.

**Nutrition Facts**

**Per Serving:**

38.1 calories; protein 0.7g 1% DV; carbohydrates 5.4g 2% DV; fat 1.8g 3% DV; cholesterol 0.6mg; sodium 875mg 35% DV.

# Hermano Roberto's Simple Salsa

**Prep:** 10 mins **Cook:** 15 mins **Additional:** 10 mins **Total:** 35 mins **Servings:** 8 **Yield:** 4 cups

**Ingredients**

- 3 medium (blank)s jalapeno peppers, or more to taste
- 1 (28 ounce) can whole peeled tomatoes with juice
- ½ teaspoon garlic salt

- ½ teaspoon ground cumin
- ¼ teaspoon ground black pepper
- ¼ teaspoon ground white pepper
- 1 tablespoon chopped cilantro

**Directions**

**Step 1**

Bring a saucepan of lightly salted water to a boil; add jalapeno peppers. Reduce heat to medium and boil peppers for 15 minutes; drain. When cool enough to handle, remove stems of peppers.

**Step 2**

Place jalapeno peppers, tomatoes, garlic salt, cumin, black pepper, white pepper, and cilantro in a blender. Blend to your desired texture, 30 seconds to 1 minute.

**Nutrition Facts**

**Per Serving:**

19.4 calories; protein 0.9g 2% DV; carbohydrates 4.4g 1% DV; fat 0.2g; cholesterolmg; sodium 253.9mg 10% DV.

# Refreshing Lemon-Ginger Dressing

**Prep:** 10 mins **Total:** 10 mins **Servings:** 16 **Yield:** 2 cups

**Ingredients**

- 1 ½ cups olive oil
- 1 ¼ cups lemon juice
- ½ cup apple cider vinegar
- ¼ cup minced fresh ginger
- ½ teaspoon salt

**Directions**

**Step 1**

Blend olive oil, lemon juice, apple cider vinegar, ginger, and salt together in a high-powered blender until smooth.

**Nutrition Facts**

**Per Serving:**

186.5 calories; protein 0.1g; carbohydrates 2g 1% DV; fat 20.3g 31% DV; cholesterolmg; sodium 73.8mg 3% DV.

# Chia Milk

**Prep:** 5 mins **Additional:** 8 hrs **Total:** 8 hrs 5 mins **Servings:** 10 **Yield:** 5 Cups

## Ingredients

- 5 cups water, divided
- ¼ cup chia seeds
- 2 tablespoons walnuts
- 2 tablespoons sesame tahini
- 1 teaspoon honey, or to taste
- 1 dash vanilla extract

## Directions

### Step 1

Combine 3 cups water, chia seeds, and walnuts in a bowl; stir to prevent clumps from forming. Let soak for 8 hours to overnight.

### Step 2

Pour chia seed mixture into a blender; add 1 cup water, tahini, honey, and vanilla extract. Cover and blend until smooth; add reminding water.

## Cook's Notes:

If I am using this recipe for soup, etc., I only add a bit of honey (milk is too sweet) and leave out the vanilla.

Toasted sesame tahini can be used instead of raw, if desired.


## Nutrition Facts

**Per Serving:**

44.8 calories; protein 1.2g 2% DV; carbohydrates 2.8g 1% DV; fat 3.5g 5% DV; cholesterolmg; sodium 7.6mg.

# Mint and Fruit Smoothie

**Prep:** 10 mins **Total:** 10 mins **Servings:** 2 **Yield:** 2 cups

**Ingredients**

- ¼ cup red seedless grapes, frozen
- ¼ cup unsweetened applesauce, or to taste
- 1 tablespoon fresh lime juice
- 3 eaches frozen strawberries
- 1 cup cubed fresh pineapple
- 3 leaf (blank)s fresh mint leaves

**Directions**

**Step 1**

Place frozen grapes, applesauce, and lime juice into a blender. Puree until smooth. Add frozen strawberries, cubed pineapple, and mint leaves. Pulse a few times until the strawberries and pineapple are in small bits.

**Nutrition Facts**

**Per Serving:**

91.6 calories; protein 0.8g 2% DV; carbohydrates 24.1g 8% DV; fat 0.3g; cholesterolmg; sodium 2.3mg.

# Best Strawberry Daiquiri

**Prep:** 10 mins **Total:** 10 mins **Servings:** 8 **Yield:** 8 servings

**Ingredients**

- 6 cups ice
- ½ cup white sugar
- 4 ounces frozen strawberries
- ⅛ cup lime juice
- ½ cup lemon juice
- ¾ cup rum
- ¼ cup lemon-lime flavored carbonated beverage

**Directions**

**Step 1**

In a blender, combine ice, sugar and strawberries. Pour in lime juice, lemon juice, rum and lemon-lime soda. Blend until smooth. Pour into glasses and serve.

**Nutrition Facts**

**Per Serving:**

109.5 calories; protein 0.1g; carbohydrates 16.3g 5% DV; fatg; cholesterolmg; sodium 6.5mg.

# Classic Old Fashioned

**Prep:** 10 mins **Total:** 10 mins **Servings:** 1 **Yield:** 1 cocktail

**Ingredients**

- 2 teaspoons simple syrup
- 1 teaspoon water
- 2 dashes bitters
- 1 cup ice cubes
- 1 (1.5 fluid ounce) jigger bourbon whiskey
- 1 slice orange
- 1 maraschino cherry

**Directions**

**Step 1**

Pour the simple syrup, water, and bitters into a whiskey glass. Stir to combine, then place the ice cubes in the glass. Pour bourbon over the ice and garnish with the orange slice and maraschino cherry.

**Nutrition Facts**

**Per Serving:**

152.8 calories; protein 0.1g; carbohydrates 11.5g 4% DV; fatg; cholesterolmg; sodium 7.6mg.

# Starbucks Caramel Frappuccino Copycat Recipe

**Prep:** 10 mins **Total:** 10 mins **Servings:** 2 **Yield:** 2 servings

**Ingredients**

- 2 cups ice
- 1 cup strong brewed coffee, cooled
- 1 cup low-fat milk
- ⅓ cup caramel sauce
- 3 tablespoons white sugar

**Directions**

**Step 1**

Blend ice, coffee, milk, caramel sauce, and sugar together in a blender on high until smooth. Pour drink into two 16-ounce glasses.

**Cook's Note:**

I made strong coffee with 2 tablespoons of ground coffee beans per cup in the coffee maker.

**Nutrition Facts**

**Per Serving:**

271.4 calories; protein 5g 10% DV; carbohydrates 60.2g 19% DV; fat 2.5g 4% DV; cholesterol 10.3mg 3% DV; sodium 241.6mg 10% DV.

# Chef John's Gazpacho

**Prep:** 45 mins **Additional:** 2 hrs **Total:** 2 hrs 45 mins **Servings:** 6 **Yield:** 6 servings

**Ingredients**

- 4 large fresh tomatoes, peeled and diced
- ½ English cucumber, peeled and finely diced
- ½ cup finely diced red bell pepper
- ¼ cup minced green onion
- 1 large jalapeno pepper, seeded and minced
- 2 cloves garlic, minced
- 1 teaspoon salt
- ½ teaspoon ground cumin
- 1 pinch dried oregano
- 1 pinch cayenne pepper, or to taste
- 1 pinch freshly ground black pepper to taste
- 1 pint cherry tomatoes
- ¼ cup extra-virgin olive oil
- 1 lime, juiced
- 1 tablespoon balsamic vinegar
- 1 teaspoon Worcestershire sauce
- 1 pinch salt and ground black pepper to taste
- 2 tablespoons thinly sliced fresh basil

**Directions**

**Step 1**

Combine diced tomatoes, cucumber, bell pepper, green onion, jalapeno, and garlic in a large bowl. Stir in salt, cumin, oregano, cayenne pepper, and black pepper.

**Step 2**

Place cherry tomatoes, olive oil, lime juice, balsamic vinegar, and Worcestershire sauce in a blender. Cover and puree until smooth. Pour pureed mixture through a strainer into the tomato-cucumber mixture; stir to combine.

**Step 3**

Place 1/3 of the tomato mixture into the blender. Cover, turn blender on, and puree until smooth. Return pureed mixture to the remaining tomato-cucumber mixture. Stir to combine. Cover and chill in refrigerator for 2 hours.

**Step 4**

Season cold soup with salt and black pepper to taste. Ladle into bowls and top with basil.

**Nutrition Facts**

**Per Serving:**

131.7 calories; protein 2g 4% DV; carbohydrates 10.5g 3% DV; fat 9.9g 15% DV; cholesterolmg; sodium 410.3mg 16% DV.

# Blueberry Smoothie

**Prep:** 5 mins **Total:** 5 mins **Servings:** 2 **Yield:** 2 servings

**Ingredients**

- 1 cup blueberries (frozen or fresh)
- 1 (8 ounce) container plain yogurt
- ¾ cup 2% reduced-fat milk
- 2 tablespoons white sugar
- ½ teaspoon vanilla extract
- ⅛ teaspoon ground nutmeg

**Directions**

**Step 1**

Blend the blueberries, yogurt, milk, sugar, vanilla, and nutmeg in a blender until frothy, scraping down the sides of the blender with a spatula occasionally. Serve immediately.

**Nutrition Facts**

**Per Serving:**

211.1 calories; protein 9.5g 19% DV; carbohydrates 35.5g 12% DV; fat 3.9g 6% DV; cholesterol 14.1mg 5% DV; sodium 117.8mg 5% DV.

# Frozen Mudslide

**Prep:** 5 mins **Total:** 5 mins **Servings:** 4 **Yield:** 4 servings

**Ingredients**

- 4 cups crushed ice
- 2 (1.5 fluid ounce) jiggers vodka
- 2 (1.5 fluid ounce) jiggers coffee flavored liqueur
- 2 (1.5 fluid ounce) jiggers Irish cream liqueur
- 2 tablespoons chocolate syrup
- ½ cup whipped cream

**Directions**

**Step 1**

In a blender, combine crushed ice, vodka, coffee liqueur and Irish cream liqueur. Drizzle in Chocolate syrup. Blend until smooth. Pour into glasses and garnish with whipped cream.

**Nutrition Facts**

**Per Serving:**

257.2 calories; protein 0.5g 1% DV; carbohydrates 25.8g 9% DV; fat 1.9g 3% DV; cholesterol 5.7mg 2% DV; sodium 26.8mg 1% DV.

# Vanilla Milkshakes without Ice Cream

**Prep:** 5 mins **Total:** 5 mins **Servings:** 4 **Yield:** 4 servings

**Ingredients**

- 12 eaches ice cubes
- 2 cups milk
- ¾ cup white sugar
- 1 dash vanilla extract, or to taste

**Directions**

**Step 1**

Blend ice, milk, sugar, and vanilla extract together in a blender until smooth.

**Nutrition Facts**

**Per Serving:**

206.8 calories; protein 4g 8% DV; carbohydrates 43.2g 14% DV; fat 2.4g 4% DV; cholesterol 9.8mg 3% DV; sodium 51.9mg 2% DV.

# Spinach and Banana Power Smoothie

**Prep:** 10 mins **Total:** 10 mins **Servings:** 1 **Yield:** 1 serving

**Ingredients**

- 1 cup plain soy milk
- ¾ cup packed fresh spinach leaves
- 1 large banana, sliced

**Directions**

**Step 1**

Blend soy milk and spinach leaves together in a blender until smooth. Add banana and pulse until thoroughly blended.

**Cook's Notes:**

You can substitute vanilla soy milk for the plain soy milk, if desired.

Most of us know how good spinach is for you. But let's be honest, no one wants to eat nothing but spinach salad every day. Bananas are truly a miracle food because you won't even taste the spinach in this smoothie! It's a great way to reap all the nutrition benefits of fresh spinach without even knowing you're eating it.

**Nutrition Facts**

**Per Serving:**

257.4 calories; protein 10.1g 20% DV; carbohydrates 47.1g 15% DV; fat 4.8g 7% DV; cholesterolmg; sodium 143.1mg 6% DV.

# Fruit and Yogurt Smoothie

**Prep:** 5 mins **Total:**5 mins **Servings:** 2 **Yield:** 2 servings

**Ingredients**

- 1 banana
- ½ cup yogurt
- 1 ½ teaspoons white sugar
- ¼ cup pineapple juice
- 1 cup strawberries
- 1 teaspoon orange juice
- 1 teaspoon milk

**Directions**

**Step 1**

Blend the banana, yogurt, sugar, pineapple juice, strawberries, orange juice, and milk in a blender until smooth.

**Nutrition Facts**

**Per Serving:**

145.6 calories; protein 4.5g 9% DV; carbohydrates 31.1g 10% DV; fat 1.4g 2% DV; cholesterol 3.7mg 1% DV; sodium 44.9mg 2% DV.

# Strawberry Lime Smoothie Pops

**Prep:** 10 mins **Additional:** 2 hrs **Total:** 2 hrs 10 mins **Servings:** 6 **Yield:** 6 -8 ice pops

**Ingredients**

- 1 cup Almond Breeze Vanilla almondmilk
- 1 cup frozen strawberries
- ½ cup vanilla Greek yogurt
- 1 tablespoon honey or maple syrup
- 1 medium banana
- ½ lime, juiced

**Directions**

**Step 1**

Blend all ingredients, then pour into ice pop molds.

**Step 2**

Freeze for at least 2 hours (or overnight).

**Note:**

You can substitute non-dairy yogurt for the vanilla Greek yogurt.

**Nutrition Facts**

**Per Serving:**

73.8 calories; protein 2.1g 4% DV; carbohydrates 16.2g 5% DV; fat 0.6g 1% DV; cholesterol 1.1mg; sodium 40mg 2% DV.

# Pineapple and Banana Smoothie

**Prep:** 3 mins **Total:** 3 mins **Servings:** 1 **Yield:** 1 smoothie

**Ingredients**

- 4 ice cubes ice cubes
- ¼ fresh pineapple - peeled, cored and cubed
- 1 large banana, cut into chunks
- 1 cup pineapple or apple juice

**Directions**

**Step 1**

Place ice cubes, pineapple, banana, and pineapple juice into the bowl of a blender. Puree on high until smooth.

**Nutrition Facts**

**Per Serving:**

312.5 calories; protein 3g 6% DV; carbohydrates 78.7g 25% DV; fat 0.9g 1% DV; cholesterolmg; sodium 10.1mg.

# Virgin Strawberry Daiquiri

**Prep:** 5 mins **Total:** 5 mins **Servings:** 1 **Yield:** 1 serving

**Ingredients**

- 2 large strawberries, hulled
- ¼ cup white sugar
- 1 tablespoon lemon juice
- ¾ cup chilled lemon-lime soda
- 4 cubes ice

## Directions

### Step 1

In the container of a blender, combine the strawberries, sugar, lemon juice and lemon-lime soda. Add the ice and blend until smooth. Pour into a fancy glass to serve.

## Nutrition Facts

**Per Serving:**

287.1 calories; protein 0.3g 1% DV; carbohydrates 74.4g 24% DV; fat 0.1g; cholesterolmg; sodium 24.6mg 1% DV.

# Very Berry Anti-Inflammatory Smoothie

**Prep:** 5 mins **Total:** 5 mins **Servings:** 2 **Yield:** 2 smoothies

## Ingredients

- 1 cup unsweetened vanilla almond milk
- 1 cup fresh cherries, pitted
- ¾ cup fresh strawberries
- ¾ cup seedless red grapes
- ½ cup frozen blueberries
- ½ teaspoon ground turmeric

## Directions

### Step 1

Pour almond milk into a high-frequency blender (such as Vitamix). Add cherries, strawberries, grapes, blueberries, and turmeric.

### Step 2

Secure lid, and turn onto variable speed 1. Increase speed to variable 10. Blend for 30 to 45 seconds.

**Nutrition Facts**

**Per Serving:**

167 calories; protein 2.4g 5% DV; carbohydrates 36.4g 12% DV; fat 2.9g 4% DV; cholesterolmg; sodium 82.3mg 3% DV.

# Cuban Mojito

**Prep:** 10 mins **Total:** 10 mins **Servings:** 2 **Yield:** 2 servings

**Ingredients**

- 2 teaspoons white sugar
- 1 lime, cut into 4 wedges
- 4 sprigs fresh mint
- ½ cup white rum
- 2 cups club soda
- 2 cups crushed ice
- 2 wedges lime, as garnish

**Directions**

**Step 1**

Place 1 teaspoon of sugar into each of two 12 ounce glasses. Squeeze the juice from a lime wedge into each glass, drop in the wedge, and add 2 sprigs of mint. Use a spoon or muddler to mash the sugar, lime juice, and mint together in the bottom of the glasses. Fill each glass about half full with crushed ice. Pour 1/4 cup rum into each glass. Fill the glasses with club soda, stir, and garnish with additional lime wedges.

**Nutrition Facts**

**Per Serving:**

158 calories; protein 0.4g 1% DV; carbohydrates 8.5g 3% DV; fat 0.1g; cholesterolmg; sodium 13.2mg 1% DV.

# Habanero Hot Sauce

**Prep:** 20 mins **Cook:** 5 mins **Total:** 25 mins **Servings:** 48 **Yield:** 3 cups

**Ingredients**

- 1 tablespoon olive oil
- 1 cup chopped carrots

- ½ cup chopped onion
- 4 cloves garlic, minced
- 5 peppers habanero peppers
- ¼ cup water
- ¼ cup lime juice
- ¼ cup white vinegar
- 1 tomato
- 1 pinch salt and ground black pepper to taste

**Directions**

**Step 1**

Heat the oil in a sauce pan over medium heat. Cook and stir the carrots, oil, onion, and garlic in the hot oil until soft, about 5 minutes; transfer to a blender. Add the whole habanero peppers, water, lime juice, white vinegar, and tomato to blender; blend until smooth. Season with salt and pepper to taste.

**Step 2**

Transfer mixture to a saucepan, and simmer for 3 to 5 minutes. This gives the sauce a more liquid consistency.

**Nutrition Facts**

**Per Serving:**

5.7 calories; protein 0.1g; carbohydrates 0.8g; fat 0.3g 1% DV; cholesterolmg; sodium 2.2mg.

# Chocolate Avocado Pudding

**Prep:** 10 mins **Additional:** 30 mins **Total:** 40 mins **Servings:** 4 **Yield:** 4 servings

**Ingredients**

- 2 large avocados - peeled, pitted, and cubed
- ½ cup unsweetened cocoa powder
- ½ cup brown sugar
- ⅓ cup coconut milk
- 2 teaspoons vanilla extract
- 1 pinch ground cinnamon

**Directions**

**Step 1**

Blend avocados, cocoa powder, brown sugar, coconut milk, vanilla extract, and cinnamon in a blender until smooth. Refrigerate pudding until chilled, about 30 minutes.

**Nutrition Facts**

**Per Serving:**

400.3 calories; protein 5.4g 11% DV; carbohydrates 45.9g 15% DV; fat 26.3g 41% DV; cholesterolmg; sodium 22.6mg 1% DV.

# Blender Hollandaise Sauce

**Prep:** 5 mins **Total:** 5 mins **Servings:** 6 **Yield:** 6 servings

## Ingredients

- 3 eaches egg yolks
- ¼ teaspoon Dijon mustard
- 1 tablespoon lemon juice
- 1 dash hot pepper sauce (e.g. Tabasco™)
- ½ cup butter

## Directions

**Step 1**

In the container of a blender, combine the egg yolks, mustard, lemon juice and hot pepper sauce. Cover, and blend for about 5 seconds.

**Step 2**

Place the butter in a glass measuring cup. Heat butter in the microwave for about 1 minute, or until completely melted and hot. Set the blender on high speed, and pour the butter into the egg yolk mixture in a thin stream. It should thicken almost immediately. Keep the sauce warm until serving by placing the blender container in a pan of hot tap water.

**Nutrition Facts**

**Per Serving:**

162.8 calories; protein 1.5g 3% DV; carbohydrates 0.6g; fat 17.5g 27% DV; cholesterol 143.1mg 48% DV; sodium 119.2mg 5% DV.

# Green Monster Smoothie

**Prep:** 5 mins **Total:** 5 mins **Servings:** 1 **Yield:** 1 smoothie

## Ingredients

- 1 cup fat-free milk
- ½ cup fat-free plain yogurt
- 1 banana, frozen and chunked
- 1 tablespoon natural peanut butter
- 2 cups fresh spinach
- 1 cup ice cubes

## Directions

### Step 1

Blend milk, yogurt, banana, peanut butter, spinach, and ice cubes until smooth.

## Nutrition Facts

**Per Serving:**

381.7 calories; protein 23.6g 47% DV; carbohydrates 55.7g 18% DV; fat 9.4g 15% DV; cholesterol 7.4mg 3% DV; sodium 328mg 13% DV.

# Oreo Milkshake

**Prep:** 10 mins **Total:** 10 mins **Servings:** 2 **Yield:** 2 servings

## Ingredients

- 3 scoops vanilla ice cream
- ¾ cup milk
- 6 cookies chocolate sandwich cookies (such as Oreo)

## Directions

### Step 1

Blend ice cream, milk, and chocolate sandwich cookies together in a blender until smooth. Pour into 2 glasses.

## Nutrition Facts

**Per Serving:**

248.9 calories; protein 5.7g 11% DV; carbohydrates 33.2g 11% DV; fat 11g 17% DV; cholesterol 21.2mg 7% DV; sodium 207.6mg 8% DV.

# Chef John's Green Goddess Dressing

**Prep:** 15 mins **Total:** 15 mins **Servings:** 16 **Yield:** 16 servings

## Ingredients

- 1 cup mayonnaise
- ¾ cup sour cream
- ⅓ cup chopped fresh flat-leaf parsley
- ⅓ cup chopped fresh tarragon
- ¼ cup chopped fresh chives
- 2 tablespoons fresh lemon juice, or more to taste
- 1 tablespoon rice vinegar
- 1 anchovy fillet
- 1 clove garlic, chopped
- 1 pinch cayenne pepper, or to taste
- 1 pinch salt and freshly ground black pepper to taste

## Directions

### Step 1

Blend mayonnaise, sour cream, parsley, tarragon, chives, lemon juice, rice vinegar, anchovy fillet, garlic, cayenne pepper, salt, and black pepper in a blender until smooth.

## Nutrition Facts

**Per Serving:**

124.3 calories; protein 0.7g 1% DV; carbohydrates 1.3g; fat 13.2g 20% DV; cholesterol 10.2mg 3% DV; sodium 103.5mg 4% DV.

# Green Goddess Dip

**Prep:** 15 mins **Additional:** 1 hr **Total:** 1 hr 15 mins **Servings:** 16 **Yield:** 2 cups

## Ingredients

- ¾ cup sour cream
- ¾ cup mayonnaise
- 2 cloves garlic, minced
- ¼ cup fresh parsley leaves

- 2 teaspoons chopped fresh tarragon
- 1 tablespoon lemon juice
- 2 anchovies anchovy fillets
- ¼ cup minced fresh chives
- 1 pinch salt and ground black pepper to taste

## Directions

## Step 1

Blend the sour cream, mayonnaise, garlic, parsley, tarragon, lemon juice, and anchovy fillets in a food processor or blender until smooth and creamy; transfer to a bowl. Gently stir the minced chives into the sour cream mixture; season with salt and pepper. Refrigerate at least 1 hour before serving.

## Nutrition Facts

## Per Serving:

99.6 calories; protein 0.7g 1% DV; carbohydrates 1.1g; fat 10.5g 16% DV; cholesterol 9.1mg 3% DV; sodium 83.3mg 3% DV.

# Easy Strawberry Vinaigrette

**Prep:** 10 mins **Total:** 10 mins **Servings:** 9 **Yield:** 9 servings

## Ingredients

- 8 ounces frozen strawberries
- 2 tablespoons honey
- 2 tablespoons apple cider vinegar
- 2 tablespoons olive oil
- ¼ teaspoon salt
- ¼ teaspoon ground black pepper

## Directions

- **Step 1**

  Blend strawberries, honey, apple cider vinegar, olive oil, salt, and black pepper together in a blender until smooth.

## Nutrition Facts

## Per Serving:

50.3 calories; protein 0.1g; carbohydrates 6.2g 2% DV; fat 3g 5% DV; cholesterolmg; sodium 65.5mg 3% DV.

# Agua Fresca de Pepino (Cucumber Limeade)

**Prep:** 5 mins **Total:** 5 mins **Servings:** 6 **Yield:** 6 cups

**Ingredients**

- 5 cups water, or to taste
- 3 eaches cucumbers, peeled and chopped
- ½ cup freshly squeezed lime juice
- ¼ cup granular sucralose sweetener (such as Splenda), or to taste

**Directions**

**Step 1**

Blend 2 cups water, cucumbers, lime juice, and 2 tablespoons sweetener together in a blender until smooth. Pour into pitcher; add remaining water. Stir in additional sweetener to taste.

**Nutrition Facts**

**Per Serving:**

5.1 calories; protein 0.1g; carbohydrates 1.7g 1% DV; fatg; cholesterolmg; sodium 6.3mg.

# The Perfect Peanut Butter Milkshake

**Prep:** 5 mins **Total:** 5 mins **Servings:** 2 **Yield:** 2 servings

**Ingredients**

- 2 cups vanilla ice cream
- ¼ cup milk
- 2 tablespoons creamy peanut butter

**Directions**

**Step 1**

Place ice cream, milk, and peanut butter in a blender; blend until smooth, 45 seconds.

**Nutrition Facts**

# Refreshing Cucumber Lemonade

**Prep:** 15 mins **Cook:** 5 mins **Additional:** 30 mins **Total:** 50 mins **Servings:** 4 **Yield:** 2 1/2 cups

**Ingredients**

- 1 cup water
- ½ cup white sugar
- 1 cucumber, sliced
- 6 eaches lemons, juiced

**Directions**

**Step 1**

Make a simple syrup by stirring the water and sugar together in a saucepan over medium heat; heat until just about to boil and the sugar has dissolved. Place in refrigerator 30 minutes, or until cool.

**Step 2**

Place the cucumber slices in a blender or food processor; blend until mashed into a pulp. Pour the cucumber pulp into a fine mesh strainer place over a bowl to catch the liquid; allow to sit until you have about 2/3 cup of liquid from the cucumber, about 15 minutes.

**Step 3**

Stir the simple syrup, cucumber liquid, and lemon juice together in a pitcher. Serve cold.

**Nutrition Facts**

**Per Serving:**

140.9 calories; protein 2.5g 5% DV; carbohydrates 45.5g 15% DV; fat 0.6g 1% DV; cholesterolmg; sodium 8.2mg.

# Enchiladas Verdes

**Prep:** 30 mins **Cook:** 30 mins **Total:** 1 hr **Servings:** 9 **Yield:** 9 enchiladas

**Ingredients**

- 2 cloves garlic

- 3 peppers serrano peppers

- 2 ¼ pounds small green tomatillos, husks removed

- 1 cup vegetable oil for frying

- 9 eaches corn tortillas

- 3 cups water

- 4 teaspoons chicken bouillon granules

- ½ store-bought rotisserie chicken, meat removed and shredded

- ¼ head iceberg lettuce, shredded

- 1 cup cilantro leaves

- 1 (8 ounce) container Mexican crema, crema fresca

- 1 cup grated cotija cheese

**Directions**

**Step 1**

Cover a large griddle with aluminum foil and preheat to medium-high.

**Step 2**

Cook the garlic, serrano peppers, and tomatillos on the hot griddle until toasted and blackened, turning occasionally, about 5 minutes for the garlic, 10 minutes for the peppers, and 15 minutes for the tomatillos. Remove to a bowl and allow to cool.

**Step 3**

Heat oil in a small, deep skillet to 350 degrees F (175 degrees C). Using kitchen tongs, fry the tortillas individually, turning them once. They shouldn't be in the hot oil for more than 5 seconds per side. Remove excess oil with paper towels and keep warm. Remember that the hotter the oil, the less that the tortillas will absorb.

**Step 4**

Place the toasted garlic, serrano peppers, tomatillos, and the water in a blender and blend until smooth; pour into a saucepan over medium heat and bring to a boil. Dissolve the chicken bouillon into the mixture, reduce heat to medium-low, and cook at a simmer until slightly thickened, about 10 minutes. The sauce shouldn't be too thick.

**Step 5**

Soak three tortillas in the sauce, one at a time, for a few seconds, fill them with shredded chicken, sprinkle the meat with some of the sauce, roll them and place them seam side down on a pasta bowl. Spoon a generous amount of sauce over them and top them with lettuce, cilantro, crema, and cotija cheese. Pour a little more sauce over the whole thing if desired. Repeat the procedure twice more. Serve immediately.

**Nutrition Facts**

**Per Serving:**

304.1 calories; protein 11.6g 23% DV; carbohydrates 20.8g 7% DV; fat 20.9g 32% DV; cholesterol 69.6mg 23% DV; sodium 222.3mg 9% DV.

# Jewel's Watermelon Margaritas

**Prep:** 10 mins **Cook:** 5 mins **Additional:** 30 mins **Total:** 45 mins **Servings:** 4 **Yield:** 4 servings

**Ingredients**

- ½ cup white sugar
- ½ cup water
- 3 strips orange zest
- 2 cups cubed seeded watermelon
- ¾ cup white tequila
- ¼ cup lime juice
- 1 pinch salt or sugar for rimming glasses
- 1 lime, cut into wedges
- 2 cups crushed ice, or as needed

**Directions**

**Step 1**

Bring 1/2 cup sugar, water, and orange zest in a small saucepan to boil, stirring constantly. Simmer until sugar is dissolved, about 3 minutes. Remove simple syrup from heat and allow to cool completely.

**Step 2**

Place watermelon in a blender or food processor. Pulse until pureed.

**Step 3**

Stir watermelon puree into a large pitcher with simple syrup, tequila, and lime juice.

**Step 4**

Place a small amount of salt or sugar into a saucer. Rub edge of margarita glasses with a lime wedge to moisten. Lightly dip the rim of the glass into the saucer to rim the glass; tap off excess salt or sugar.

**Step 5**

Fill rimmed glasses with crushed ice; pour margarita mixture into glasses and garnish with lime wedges to serve.


**Cook's Notes:**

Fill sugar or salt rimmed glasses with crushed ice, then pour margarita mixture over top. Garnish with a lime wedge.

To make a frozen version, crush 1.5 cups of ice in a high-quality blender. Add watermelon, tequila, lime juice, and simple syrup and blend until smooth.

**Nutrition Facts**

**Per Serving:**

241.4 calories; protein 0.9g 2% DV; carbohydrates 37.5g 12% DV; fat 0.2g; cholesterolmg; sodium 41.9mg 2% DV.

# Easy Mango Banana Smoothie

**Prep:** 10 mins **Total:** 10 mins **Servings:** 8 **Yield:** 8 servings

**Ingredients**

- 2 eaches mangos - peeled, seeded, and sliced
- 2 medium (7" to 7-7/8" long)s bananas
- 2 cups vanilla yogurt
- 2 cups milk

**Directions**

**Step 1**

Blend mangos, banana, vanilla yogurt, and milk in a blender until smooth.

**Nutrition Facts**

**Per Serving:**

133.2 calories; protein 5.5g 11% DV; carbohydrates 24.4g 8% DV; fat 2.2g 3% DV; cholesterol 7.9mg 3% DV; sodium 66.5mg 3% DV.

# Simple Cantaloupe Smoothie

**Prep:** 10 mins **Total:** 10 mins **Servings:** 1 **Yield:** 1 smoothie

**Ingredients**

- 1 cup vanilla yogurt (such as Dannon Light and Fit)
- ½ cup orange juice
- ½ cup sliced cantaloupe
- 4 eaches ice cubes, crushed, or as needed

**Directions**

**Step 1**

Blend yogurt, orange juice, cantaloupe, and ice cubes in a blender until smooth, about 30 seconds.

**Nutrition Facts**

**Per Serving:**

291.3 calories; protein 13.6g 27% DV; carbohydrates 53.2g 17% DV; fat 3.5g 5% DV; cholesterol 12.3mg 4% DV; sodium 178.3mg 7% DV.

# Classic Frozen Strawberry Margarita

**Prep:** 10 mins **Total:** 10 mins **Servings:** 1 **Yield:** 1 serving

**Ingredients**

- ¼ cup sliced fresh strawberries
- 1 ½ fluid ounces tequila
- 1 fluid ounce lime juice
- ½ fluid ounce triple sec
- 1 teaspoon white sugar, or to taste
- 1 cup ice cubes
- 1 wedge lime
- 1 teaspoon white sugar

**Directions**

**Step 1**

Blend strawberries, tequila, lime juice, triple sec, and 1 teaspoon sugar in blender to combine, about 10 seconds. Add ice cubes; blend on high until the ice is crushed, about 15 seconds.

**Step 2**

Rub lime wedge around the rim of a glass. Spread 1 teaspoon sugar onto a plate. Dip glass rim in sugar to coat. Pour margarita into the glass.

**Nutrition Facts**

**Per Serving:**

206.2 calories; protein 0.4g 1% DV; carbohydrates 21.3g 7% DV; fat 0.2g; cholesterolmg; sodium 2.5mg.

# Simple Cucumber Soup

**Prep:** 15 mins **Cook:** 25 mins **Total:** 40 mins **Servings:** 3 **Yield:** 3 servings

**Ingredients**

- 1 tablespoon butter, or more to taste
- 1 tablespoon olive oil
- 1 small yellow onion, chopped
- 1 large clove garlic, minced
- 2 large English cucumbers, peeled and thinly sliced
- 2 small zucchinis, peeled and thinly sliced
- 3 cups vegetable broth

**Directions**

**Step 1**

Melt butter with the oil in a large saucepan over medium-high heat. Cook and stir onion and garlic in the butter mixture until tender, 3 to 5 minutes. Add cucumber and zucchini slices; cook and stir until softened, 2 to 3 minutes. Pour vegetable broth over the mixture; bring to a boil, reduce heat to medium-low, and let simmer until the vegetables are cooked through, 20 to 25 minutes. Remove from heat and cool a few minutes.

**Step 2**

Pour soup into a blender no more than half full. Cover and hold lid in place with a towel; pulse a few times before leaving on to blend. Puree in batches until smooth.

**Nutrition Facts**

**Per Serving:**

150.5 calories; protein 3.4g 7% DV; carbohydrates 15g 5% DV; fat 9.3g 14% DV; cholesterol 10.2mg 3% DV; sodium 500.2mg 20% DV.

# Strawberry Banana Protein Smoothie

**Prep:** 10 mins **Total:** 10 mins **Servings:** 1 **Yield:** 1 smoothie

## Ingredients

- 1 banana
- 1 ¼ cups sliced fresh strawberries
- 10 almonds whole almonds
- 2 tablespoons water
- 1 cup ice cubes
- 3 tablespoons chocolate flavored protein powder

## Directions

**Step 1**

Place the banana, strawberries, almonds, and water into a blender. Blend to mix, then add the ice cubes and puree until smooth. Add the protein powder, and continue mixing until evenly incorporated, about 30 seconds.

**Nutrition Facts**

**Per Serving:**

349.4 calories; protein 21g 42% DV; carbohydrates 53.2g 17% DV; fat 8.1g 12% DV; cholesterolmg; sodium 194.5mg 8% DV.

# Healthy Berry and Spinach Smoothie

**Prep:** 10 mins **Total:** 10 mins **Servings:** 4 **Yield:** 4 servings

## Ingredients

- 2 cups frozen berries
- 1 cup plain yogurt
- ½ cup orange juice
- ¼ cup fresh spinach, or to taste
- 5 medium (1-1/4" dia)s strawberries

## Directions

### Step 1

Blend berries, yogurt, orange juice, spinach, and strawberries together in a blender until smooth.

## Nutrition Facts

**Per Serving:**

87.8 calories; protein 4.1g 8% DV; carbohydrates 17.3g 6% DV; fat 1.3g 2% DV; cholesterol 3.7mg 1% DV; sodium 44.8mg 2% DV.

# Indian Fish Curry

**Prep:** 20 mins **Cook:** 35 mins **Additional:** 30 mins **Total:** 1 hr 25 mins **Servings:** 4 **Yield:** 4 servings

## Ingredients

- 2 teaspoons Dijon mustard
- 1 teaspoon ground black pepper
- ½ teaspoon salt
- 2 tablespoons canola oil
- 4 eaches white fish fillets
- 1 onion, coarsely chopped
- 4 cloves garlic, roughly chopped
- 1 (1 inch) piece fresh ginger root, peeled and chopped
- 5 eaches cashew halves

- 1 tablespoon canola oil
- 2 teaspoons cayenne pepper, or to taste
- ½ teaspoon ground turmeric
- 1 teaspoon ground cumin
- 1 teaspoon ground coriander
- 1 teaspoon salt
- 1 teaspoon white sugar
- ½ cup chopped tomato
- ¼ cup vegetable broth
- ¼ cup chopped fresh cilantro

## Directions

### Step 1

Mix the mustard, pepper, 1/2 teaspoon salt, and 2 tablespoons of canola oil in a shallow bowl. Add the fish fillets, turning to coat. Marinate the fish in the refrigerator for 30 minutes.

### Step 2

Combine the onion, garlic, ginger, and cashews in a blender or food processor and pulse until the mixture forms a paste.

### Step 3

Preheat an oven to 350 degrees F (175 degrees C).

### Step 4

Heat 1 tablespoon of canola oil in a skillet over medium-low heat. Stir in the prepared paste; cook and stir for a minute or two. Add the cayenne pepper, turmeric, cumin, coriander, 1 teaspoon salt, and sugar. Cook and stir for an additional five minutes. Stir in the chopped tomato and vegetable broth.

### Step 5

Arrange the fish fillets in a baking dish, discarding any extra marinade. Top the fish with the sauce, cover the baking dish, and bake in the preheated oven until the fish flakes easily with a fork, about 30 minutes. Garnish with chopped cilantro.

## Cook's Notes

You can use frozen fish fillets for this recipe; thaw them before use. Decrease the amount of cayenne pepper if you prefer a less spicy dish.

# Sopa de Fideos

**Prep:** 15 mins **Cook:** 15 mins **Total:** 30 mins **Servings:** 4 **Yield:** 4 servings

**Ingredients**

- 1 (14.5 ounce) can diced tomatoes
- 1 small onion, chopped
- 1 large clove garlic, coarsely chopped
- 2 tablespoons olive oil
- 1 (7 ounce) package fideo pasta, uncooked
- 3 (14.5 ounce) cans chicken broth
- 1 pinch freshly ground black pepper to taste
- 1 pinch coarse salt to taste
- 1 tablespoon chopped fresh cilantro

**Directions**

**Step 1**

Place the tomatoes, onion, and garlic into a blender, and pulse several times to get the mixture moving; blend until smooth, 30 seconds to 1 minute.

**Step 2**

Heat the olive oil in a skillet over medium-low heat, and stir in the pasta. Fry the pasta gently, stirring often, until the pasta is golden brown, 2 to 5 minutes. Remove from heat.

**Step 3**

Pour the tomato mixture into a large saucepan, and stir in chicken broth and noodles. Bring to a boil, and reduce heat to medium low; simmer until the noodles are tender, 7 to 8 minutes. Season to taste with salt and black pepper, and stir in the cilantro; simmer 2 more minutes to cook cilantro.

**Cook's Note**

You can substitute angel hair pasta, broken into small pieces, for fideo.

**Nutrition Facts**

**Per Serving:**

291.5 calories; protein 9.3g 19% DV; carbohydrates 44g 14% DV; fat 8.2g 13% DV; cholesterol 6.8mg 2% DV; sodium 1507mg 60% DV.

# Pesto Egg Salad

**Prep:** 20 mins **Total:** 20 mins **Servings:** 4 **Yield:** 4 servings

**Ingredients**

- 6 eaches hard-boiled eggs, peeled and chopped
- 1 ½ tablespoons olive oil mayonnaise (such as Hellmann's), divided, or more to taste
- 3 cloves garlic, finely chopped
- 2 cups packed fresh basil
- ⅓ cup freshly grated Parmesan cheese, plus more for serving
- ¼ cup pine nuts
- ¼ cup olive oil
- 1 pinch Himalayan salt, or to taste
- 1 pinch ground white pepper, or to taste
- ¼ cup finely chopped green onions

**Directions**

**Step 1**

Mix together boiled eggs and half of the mayonnaise. Set aside.

**Step 2**

Blend garlic, basil, Parmesan cheese, pine nuts, olive oil, salt, and pepper together until smooth in a blender. Combine 2 tablespoons of this pesto mixture, eggs, and remaining mayonnaise together; mix well to desired consistency.

**Step 3**

Top with green onions, Parmesan cheese, salt, and pepper.

**Nutrition Facts**

**Per Serving:**

360.5 calories; protein 15g 30% DV; carbohydrates 4.4g 1% DV; fat 31.9g 49% DV; cholesterol 325.8mg 109% DV; sodium 307.2mg 12% DV.

# Healthy Chocolate Smoothie

**Prep:** 10 mins **Total:** 10 mins **Servings:** 2 **Yield:** 2 smoothies

## Ingredients

- 2 eaches very ripe bananas
- 6 eaches ice cubes
- 1 cup milk
- 1 ½ tablespoons unsweetened cocoa powder
- 1 tablespoon peanut butter
- 1 teaspoon vanilla extract

## Directions

### Step 1

Blend bananas, ice cubes, milk, cocoa powder, peanut butter, and vanilla extract together in a blender on high speed until smooth.

## Nutrition Facts

**Per Serving:**

229.3 calories; protein 8.1g 16% DV; carbohydrates 36.7g 12% DV; fat 7.4g 12% DV; cholesterol 9.8mg 3% DV; sodium 91.5mg 4% DV.

# Creamy Banana Milkshake

**Prep:** 10 mins **Total:** 10 mins **Servings:** 1 **Yield:** 1 serving

## Ingredients

- 1 cup milk
- 1 scoop vanilla ice cream
- 1 ripe banana
- 1 pinch ground cinnamon, or to taste
- 2 tablespoons whipped cream, or more to taste
- 1 tablespoon caramel topping

## Directions

### Step 1

Combine milk, ice cream, banana, and cinnamon in a blender; blend on low speed until consistency of a thick milkshake. Pour milkshake into a cup and top with whipped cream and drizzled caramel.

**Nutrition Facts**

**Per Serving:**

338.8 calories; protein 10.6g 21% DV; carbohydrates 58.4g 19% DV; fat 8.9g 14% DV; cholesterol 33.5mg 11% DV; sodium 197.5mg 8% DV.

# Thai Red Curry Paste

**Prep:** 15 mins **Total:** 15 mins **Servings:** 4 **Yield:** 1 cup

## Ingredients

- 5 peppers dried red chile peppers, or to taste
- 2 eaches onions, cut into chunks
- 2 tablespoons chopped fresh cilantro
- 1 tablespoon vegetable oil, or more as needed
- 1 tablespoon chopped garlic
- 1 tablespoon ground coriander
- 2 teaspoons lemon zest
- 2 teaspoons ground cumin
- 2 teaspoons shrimp paste
- 2 teaspoons paprika
- 1 teaspoon whole black peppercorns
- 1 teaspoon lemon grass powder
- 1 teaspoon ground turmeric
- 1 teaspoon salt

## Directions

### Step 1

Blend chile peppers, onions, cilantro, oil, garlic, coriander, lemon zest, cumin, shrimp paste, paprika, peppercorns, lemon grass, turmeric, and salt together in a blender until a smooth, paste-like consistency is reached.

**Nutrition Facts**

**Per Serving:**

102.8 calories; protein 2.6g 5% DV; carbohydrates 15g 5% DV; fat 4.3g 7% DV; cholesterol 1.6mg 1% DV; sodium 592.6mg 24% DV.

# Roasted Acorn Squash Soup

**Prep: 20 mins Cook: 1 hr 5 mins Total: 1 hr 25 mins Servings: 6 Yield: 6 servings**

**Ingredients**

- 2 medium (blank)s acorn squash, halved and seeded
- ½ cup water, as needed
- 3 tablespoons unsalted butter
- 1 large sweet onion, chopped
- 1 large carrot, peeled and chopped
- 1 clove garlic, minced
- 3 ½ cups low-sodium chicken stock
- ¼ cup half-and-half
- ½ teaspoon ground nutmeg
- ½ teaspoon ground cinnamon
- 1 pinch salt and ground black pepper to taste

**Directions**

**Step 1**

Preheat oven to 400 degrees F (200 degrees C).

**Step 2**

Put squash into a baking dish with the cut side down. Pour enough water into the baking dish to cover the bottom.

**Step 3**

Bake in preheated oven until the flesh of the squash is easily pricked with a fork, about 45 minutes. Remove from oven and allow to cool until squash can be handled. Scoop flesh into a bowl and set aside.

**Step 4**

Melt butter in a pot over medium-high heat. Cook onion, carrot, and garlic in melted butter until soft, 5 to 7 minutes. Pour chicken stock into the pot; add the squash.

**Step 5**

Bring the mixture to a simmer and cook for 20 minutes.

**Step 6**

Pour mixture into a blender no more than half full. Cover and hold lid down; pulse a few times before leaving on to blend. Puree in batches until smooth and return to pot.

**Step 7**

Stir half-and-half, nutmeg, and cinnamon through the blended soup; season with salt and pepper. Thin the soup with water if desired.

**Nutrition Facts**

**Per Serving:**

155.4 calories; protein 3.9g 8% DV; carbohydrates 21g 7% DV; fat 7.5g 12% DV; cholesterol 21.3mg 7% DV; sodium 125.3mg 5% DV.

# Menny's Blueberry Barbecue Sauce

**Prep:** 10 mins **Cook:** 15 mins **Total:** 25 mins **Servings:** 12 **Yield:** 12 servings

## Ingredients

- 2 teaspoons olive oil
- 1 onion, chopped
- 3 cloves garlic, minced
- 1 (1/2 inch) piece fresh ginger, grated
- 3 cups blueberries
- ¼ cup real maple syrup
- 2 tablespoons cider vinegar
- 2 tablespoons balsamic vinegar
- 2 tablespoons Worcestershire sauce
- 2 tablespoons molasses
- ½ teaspoon lemon juice
- ½ teaspoon ground cinnamon
- ½ teaspoon ground cumin
- ½ teaspoon chili powder
- ½ teaspoon paprika
- ½ teaspoon smoked paprika
- ½ teaspoon salt
- ½ teaspoon ground black pepper

**Directions**

**Step 1**

Heat olive oil in a skillet over medium heat; cook and stir onion, garlic, and ginger until onion is softened, about 8 minutes. Add blueberries, maple syrup, cider vinegar, balsamic vinegar, Worcestershire sauce, molasses, lemon juice, cinnamon, cumin, chili powder, paprika, smoked paprika, salt, and black pepper; stir to combine. Simmer over medium-low heat until sauce is slightly reduced and bubbling, 5 to 7 minutes.

**Step 2**

Remove skillet from heat; cool slightly. Pour sauce into a blender no more than half full. Cover and hold lid down; pulse a few times before leaving on to blend. Puree in batches until smooth.

**Nutrition Facts**

**Per Serving:**

65.5 calories; protein 0.5g 1% DV; carbohydrates 14.6g 5% DV; fat 1g 2% DV; cholesterolmg; sodium 129.5mg 5% DV.

# The Best Post Workout Shake

**Prep:** 10 mins **Total:** 10 mins **Servings:** 1 **Yield:** 1 shake

**Ingredients**

- 1 scoop whey protein powder
- 1 tablespoon flax seed meal
- 1 tablespoon unsweetened cocoa powder
- 1 teaspoon brown sugar
- 1 cup unsweetened almond milk
- 1 banana
- ½ cup frozen mixed berries
- 1 tablespoon smooth peanut butter

**Directions**

**Step 1**

Layer protein powder, flax meal, cocoa powder, and brown sugar in a blender; add almond milk, banana, berries, and peanut butter. Blend until smooth, about 1 minute.

Cook's Note:

For thicker shake, use low-fat milk.

**Nutrition Facts**

**Per Serving:**

492.7 calories; protein 29.2g 58% DV; carbohydrates 66.8g 22% DV; fat 16.5g 25% DV; cholesterolmg; sodium 207.7mg 8% DV.

# Banana Peanut Butter Smoothie

**Prep:** 10 mins **Total:** 10 mins **Servings:** 1 **Yield:** 1 smoothie

**Ingredients**

- 1 cup unsweetened almond milk
- 1 frozen banana, sliced
- ½ cup ice, or as needed
- 2 tablespoons powdered peanut butter
- 1 tablespoon cocoa powder
- 1 teaspoon cinnamon

**Directions**

**Step 1**

Blend almond milk, banana, ice, peanut butter, cocoa powder, and cinnamon together in a blender until smooth.

**Nutrition Facts**

**Per Serving:**

232 calories; protein 7.5g 15% DV; carbohydrates 46.3g 15% DV; fat 4.8g 7% DV; cholesterolmg; sodium 232.4mg 9% DV.

# Tahini

**Prep:** 10 mins **Cook:** 10 mins **Total:** 20 mins **Servings:** 10 **Yield:** 10 servings

**Ingredients**

- 1 cup sesame seeds

- ¼ cup olive oil, or as needed

**Directions**

**Step 1**

Preheat oven to 350 degrees F (175 degrees C).

**Step 2**

Spread sesame seeds onto a baking sheet.

**Step 3**

Bake in the preheated oven until seeds are fragrant, stirring every few minutes, 10 to 12 minutes.

**Step 4**

Transfer toasted seeds to a blender and add olive oil. Blend until completely smooth, adding additional oil if needed. Refrigerate in a sealed container.

**Nutrition Facts**

**Per Serving:**

130.2 calories; protein 2.6g 5% DV; carbohydrates 3.4g 1% DV; fat 12.6g 19% DV; cholesterolmg; sodium 1.7mg.

# Watermelon Milkshake

**Prep:** 10 mins **Total:** 10 mins **Servings:** 4 **Yield:** 4 servings

**Ingredients**

- 1 ½ cups diced watermelon

- 2 ¼ cups milk

- 2 teaspoons white sugar

**Directions**

**Step 1**

Process the watermelon and milk together in a blender until smooth. Add the sugar and blend another 10 seconds to incorporate. Serve immediately.

**Nutrition Facts**

# Green Power Mojito Smoothie

**Prep:** 10 mins **Total:** 10 mins **Servings:** 4 **Yield:** 48 ounces

## Ingredients

- 3 cups ice cubes, or as desired
- 2 cups baby spinach leaves, or to taste
- 1 (7 ounce) can crushed pineapple
- ½ cup water, or to taste
- 1 banana, broken into chunks
- 1 orange, peeled and segmented
- 10 leaf (blank)s fresh mint leaves, or more to taste
- 1 lemon, juiced
- 1 lime, juiced

## Directions

### Step 1

Blend ice, spinach, pineapple, water, banana, orange, mint, lemon juice, and lime juice in a blender until smooth.

Cook's Note:

Try a variety of 'power greens' with or in place of the spinach.

## Nutrition Facts

**Per Serving:**

93.5 calories; protein 1.5g 3% DV; carbohydrates 24.2g 8% DV; fat 0.3g; cholesterolmg; sodium 14mg 1% DV.